Trade Secrets from Use What You Have® Decorating

Trade Secrets from Use What You Have® Decorating

Lauri Ward

G. P. PUTNAM'S SONS
New York

G. P. Putnam's Sons
Publishers Since 1838
a member of
Penguin Putnam Inc.
375 Hudson Street
New York, NY 10014

Library of Congress Cataloging-in-Publication Data

Ward, Lauri.
Trade secrets from Use What You Have® decorating /
Lauri Ward ; illustrations by Travis Mong.
p.   cm.
ISBN 0-399-14809-4
1. Interior decoration—History—20th century.   I. Title.

NK2115 .W195   2002   2001048726
747.2'049—dc21

Printed in the United States of America

1   3   5   7   9   10   8   6   4   2

This book is printed on acid-free paper. ♾

Book design by Amanda Dewey

HOME IS WHERE THE HEART IS.

To my mother, Hedy, and my grandmother, Lillian,
who both had hearts of gold.

Acknowledgments

My sincere gratitude goes to my agent and friend, Liv Blumer, who kept me moving and always knew when to step in with her special brand of smart and thoughtful guidance. My deep appreciation to John Duff, for his vision of how to give readers a really useful decorating book and for his graciousness and good taste. Special thanks to Catriona Stuart, my assistant, for her loyal efforts in organizing this book for many months, and to Travis Mong for his fine illustrations. I am grateful to the talented people at Penguin Putnam for doing a terrific job: Cathy Fox, Bonnie Soodek, Michelle Sembler, Lisa Amoroso, Claire Vaccaro, Amanda Dewey, and Tess Bresnan. Thanks to Judy Kern, whose skills helped pull the manuscript together, and to the Use-What-You-Have® team, especially Rita Grossman for her suggestions and Suzanne Cummings for her help, to the members of the Interior Refiners Network who are a continual source of inspiration, and to everyone at the Karpfinger Agency. And to my dearest, Joe and Tracy: I am so thankful for all the love and laughter we share every day.

Contents

Trade Secrets from Use What You Have® Decorating

✦

Introduction

When I founded Use-What-You-Have® Interiors in 1981, my goal was simple: to provide decorating help for people who wanted a pretty home that they could be proud of but who didn't want to spend a fortune, throw out all their furniture, rip their entire house apart, and live in a construction site for several months. I wanted to reach people who had never worked with an interior designer but who needed help solving design problems that were preventing them from being completely comfortable in their own homes.

As demand for the Use What You Have® concept grew, I realized it wasn't only homeowners and apartment dwellers all over the country who wanted help; many people also wanted to learn how to set up a one-day decorating business. I began training decorators in my methods, and the Interior Refiners Network was born. Today IRN has members all over the United States as well as in Canada and Europe.

But what about all the people who still didn't have access to an in-person consultation? Those are the people for whom I wrote *Use What You Have*® *Decorating*. I have always believed that reliable decorating advice should be available to everyone, and there is no doubt about it, *Use What You Have*® *Decorating* has struck a chord. Since its publication in 1998, hundreds of spatially challenged people have telephoned, sent e-mail, and written letters with enthusiastic anecdotes about the impact the Use What You Have® philosophy has had on their homes and their lives. They are thrilled to learn how simple the principles are to understand and how quickly they can effect dramatic changes in their houses and apartments. By revealing the ten most common decorating mistakes and their solutions, that book enabled thousands of people to become their own decorators, transform their own spaces, and live more comfortably. And now those thousands of converts to the "quicker, faster, cheaper" approach to decorating are asking for even more instant interior gratification.

Writing *Use What You Have*® *Decorating* was a great experience, but space limitations meant that it was necessary for me to leave many questions unanswered. Now, in *Trade Secrets,* I finally have the opportunity to provide those answers. And I hope to give you, my readers, even more alternatives to the "mansions for you and me" genre of fantasy decorating books while also allowing you to build on what you've already learned.

Learning is key to the Use What You Have® philosophy. It is not about thumbing through dozens of glossy color photos that look nothing like your home; rather it's about giving you the information that will allow you to make your own space look and feel the way you want it to.

But I am not going to assume you have read *Use What You Have*® *Decorating*. Throughout this book, I will review important principles that will serve both as reminders to past readers and as a foundation for those of you who are learning them for the first time. You'll find that the tips in each chapter run from the general, or the most basic, to the specific. That's because this is the order to follow whenever you're tackling a redecorating project. Start with the basics—the walls, the floors, the lighting, and the windows—the "shell" of the house, and move on to the details—the furniture, the art, the accessories, and finishing touches.

A caution for all women: Do *not* assume you should know how to decorate your home simply because you were born with two "X" chromosomes. I have met too many women who believed there must be something wrong with them because they couldn't figure out how to light their living room or hang the artwork in their bedroom. Others felt bad because their sister or neighbor had a "knack" for decorating and they didn't. This book is not about comparing yourself to your friends or family; it's about making *you* happier in your home.

So, readers old and new, wherever you live, whatever your age or income level, I hope this compendium of tips, lists, and real-life scenarios will help improve the quality of your life and supply you with useful decorating advice you can implement easily, without draining your bank account or taking too much time away from other important things in your life.

The Redecorator's
Timeline Game

"Where do I start?"

This is possibly the most frequently asked question I hear from clients. And while each redecorating project has its own challenges, there are some universal guidelines that will help you sort out the order in which you will do things and avoid the chaos that comes with trying to do everything at once.

"High to low / big to small"

This phrase should become your mantra when you redecorate. Work from the ceiling to the floor and from the biggest project to the smallest. This means starting with the shell of your rooms—ceilings, walls, and floors—and going from there to the smallest details of placing objects on a table.

Planning

As eager as you might be to get started, keep in mind the carpenter's axiom: Measure twice, cut once. If you think ahead, you will save time, money, and a lot of grief. Use the following timeline as your guide to a happier and saner redecoration.

Phase I: Preparing the Shell

Clean Out and Clean Up

Get rid of the clutter—furnishings, artwork, and accessories that are useless, too old or out-of-date to be salvaged, or simply don't fit anymore. (And don't forget all that stuff packed away in closets and drawers!)

The Big Ten

Review the "Ten Most Common Decorating Mistakes" in chapter 1. Determine what will go where. (If you can't find a place for something in your plan, go back to step one.) Review the mistakes now to avoid repeating them in the future.

Wish List

Make a list of additional items—furniture, lamps, rugs, etc.—now, that we will need later, so you can anticipate sales and/or delivery times.

Hammer and Saw

Decide what, if any, structural changes or building needs to be done. Now is the time to design and install built-ins or accommodate renovations. And remember, everything at this stage takes longer than you think it will—no matter what your contractor tells you!

Wires and Plugs

Design and install new wiring for lighting and other electrical needs in walls and ceilings.

Window and Floor Coverings

Select and order new window treatments and rugs or have old items cleaned while walls and floors are being done. New carpeting can be ordered now for later delivery.

Furniture Restoration

Send out furniture to be reupholstered, repaired, or refinished. Order slipcovers or new pieces and have them delivered once the major paint and renovation work is finished.

Walls and Ceilings

Repair, prepare, pai nt, and/or paper walls and ceilings.

Floors

Repair, refinish, and/or replace wood floors. Regrout, replace, or clean tile. Clean carpets.

Phase II: Putting It Back Together

Window and Floor Coverings

Hang new or cleaned window treatments; place rugs or lay new carpeting.

Furniture

Arrange furniture. (See chapters 1 and 2.)

Art

Choose, reframe as needed, and hang art, mirrors, etc. Plan for rotating pieces. (See chapter 8.)

Accessories

Select and place accessories, including decorative objects, lamps, books, etc. (See chapters 8 and 13.)

CHAPTER 1

The Ten Most Common Decorating Mistakes

Having a home as beautiful as those you see in decorating magazines does not have to be a fantasy. Everyone can learn how to redecorate their rooms simply by becoming aware of the ten most common decorating mistakes and how to prevent or correct them. You will probably want to refer to these guidelines time and again throughout your redecorating project. Here are the mistakes to look out for, and my suggestions for correcting them:

1. Not defining your priorities

Determine your needs and budget, based on whether you own or rent and who lives in your house.

2. An uncomfortable conversation area

Can people sit and face one another when chatting? Do they have to raise their voices to be heard? Create the ideal, a U-shaped conversation area, and avoid the least comfortable, the L-shaped configuration.

3. Poor furniture placement

Avoid pressing all your furniture up against the walls. But make sure you can walk through the room unobstructed by furniture.

4. A room that is off balance

Always consider the height and size of furnishings. Avoid having all heavy or tall pieces on one side of the room. For example, you can balance an armoire on one side of the room with an indoor tree diagonally across from it on the other side.

5. Furniture of different heights

Try to keep your upholstered pieces at one height, and hang your art at approximately the same level, to prevent a visual "roller coaster."

6. A room that lacks a cohesive look

Using pairs—of chairs, lamps, etc.—is the fastest way to give any room a pulled-together look.

7. Ignoring the room's focal point

A fireplace, a window with a view, a large painting, or a grouping of smaller paintings are all eye-catching, and each can serve as a focal point. Once you have established what the focal point is, play it up.

8. Improper use of artwork

Hang all your art three inches lower than you think it should be, instead of at "eye level" (it works!), and leave one wall blank in every room to give the eye a place to rest.

9. Ineffective use of accessories

Keep collections together. Rotate your accessories seasonally. Less is more when it comes to knickknacks.

10. Using lighting incorrectly

Be sure that each room has both general illumination and task lighting, and that your art and accessories have accent lighting whenever possible.

CHAPTER 2

All About Furniture

Figuring out where to put your furniture is like trying to complete a jigsaw puzzle. What you imagine in your head or on a floor plan often doesn't come out the way you'd hoped it might. That's when "decorating anxiety" usually starts to kick in.

Fortunately, there are some basic rules that will help you avoid aggravation and save you both time and money.

1. When arranging your seating, a U-shaped conversation area is ideal, while an L-shaped area is always uncomfortable. A sofa and a matching pair of chairs easily establish a comfortable U-shaped configuration that allows everyone who is seated to have an intimate chat facing everyone else. A sectional sofa or a sofa and loveseat that form an L-shape, on the other hand, make everyone "twist and shout" when trying to have a conversation.

2. Avoid pressing the furniture against opposite walls. This common decorating mistake makes conversation awkward because it creates "screaming distance."

Floating furniture in the center of a room, such as a pair of loveseats or sofas facing one another, or a U-shaped group around a fireplace, fosters a sense of intimacy.

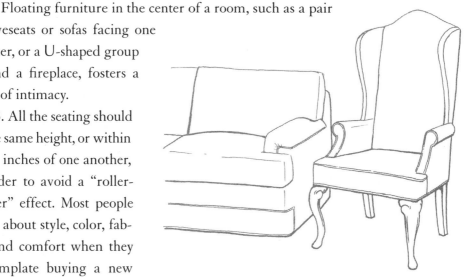

3. All the seating should be the same height, or within a few inches of one another, in order to avoid a "roller-coaster" effect. Most people think about style, color, fabric, and comfort when they contemplate buying a new sofa or chairs. But they never think about the height of their seating. The issue of height is especially important if you are buying a pair of chairs to go with a sofa or vice versa.

Grandma's Rocker and other Family Heirlooms

Many of us are inheriting furnishings from parents and grandparents, and trying to figure out which pieces we should keep and which we should sell or donate to charity.

But before you start discarding old or inherited pieces in search of your distinctive "look," consider whether you can reconfigure, reupholster, or relocate what you already have on hand. (Many tips and ideas throughout this book are based on the fundamental principle of "use what you have®.")

Eclectic, Not Frenetic

If you are afraid of mixing and matching different periods and styles without the help of a professional, fear no more. Just follow these three simple rules:

1. Color: Match your wood finishes as closely as possible. Use all dark, all light, or all middle-range stained wood pieces together.

2. Scale: Keep furnishings of similar size together.

3. Fabrics: Coordinate the color scheme of your upholstered pieces, so that everything looks tied together, even if they are of different periods. (Note: This does not necessarily mean reupholstering every piece in the *same* fabric, although you might use this technique for slipcovers. If you have only two or three pieces—sofa, chair, and ottoman—using the identical fabric can work, but it's preferable for the chair and ottoman to match and the sofa to be in a second, coordinated fabric. Watch out for overblown patterns that will be hard to work with.)

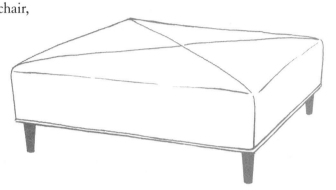

Put Your Best Foot Forward

Show off your best pieces and camouflage those that are less costly. If you have a painted, wooden storage piece made of pine or another inexpensive wood, paint it the same color as the walls, but with a semigloss finish. The piece will blend in with the background, the room will appear larger, and the eye will focus on your finer wood pieces of furniture.

Focusing Attention

Almost every living room has at least one natural focal point. If yours has a fireplace, that will no doubt be it. Other focal points might be a picture window with a wonderful view or a pair of French doors. Whatever the focal point of your room, be sure you arrange your furniture to take advantage of it—since everyone's eyes will naturally be drawn to it in any case.

Making It Your Own

I was hired to redecorate the home of a woman in her forties who had lived with her mother for the previous ten years. The mother had passed away a few months prior to the consultation, and when I arrived, it was obvious that nothing in the apartment had been moved or changed in decades. In fact, there was no sign that the residence had been inhabited by anyone but the woman's mother.

My client explained that her mother had had a "strong" personality and very definite ideas about how things should look. It was evident that her notions had prevailed, but now that her mother was gone, the younger woman began to realize that she had been living in a time warp with furnishings she mostly didn't like and didn't use. And she felt that her surroundings were having a negative impact on her entire life.

Unsure where to begin, she was seeking support and my assurance that she was doing the "right" thing. I suggested that we start with the living room, assessing *her* lifestyle and deciding which furnishings she liked and which she did not. Soon it became clear that we would be able to use the good basic pieces, such as the sofa and club chairs, which only needed reupholstering, but many of the other furnishings would be given away or sold.

Room by room, we quickly rearranged all the furniture, lighting, and artwork we had earmarked as "keepers," and suddenly, the whole house began to move into the 21st century.

My client smiled brightly and said, "This is the first time I have ever felt comfortable here! Who knows, maybe I'll even be able to eat in the living room while I watch TV." Then she looked up at the ceiling and said, "Don't roll over, Mom."

Moving "Magic"

Trying to figure out the perfect placement for your furniture? You can use what professionals use when you need to move a heavy piece. "Magic Sliders" come in a variety of sizes and shapes and make it possible to move heavy furnishings for cleaning or rearranging. (See Resources.)

Two-Part Harmony

To create a beautiful room, think in pairs. If you have a good piece without a mate, find it a partner.

- End tables will complement each other if they are of similar size and finish.
- Two different upholstered chairs can be slip-covered in the same fabric to create a pair, so long as they are of similar height and scale.
- Fit two lamps of similar height and style with new, matching shades.
- If your windows or doors are of different sizes and heights and are not evenly spaced, you'll need a minimum of three pairs—of chairs, lamps, or end tables—to create a sense of balance and make the room aesthetically more pleasing.

Saving Your Sanity While Buying a Sofa

A sofa is definitely one of the most important purchases you'll make for your home. Not only are sofas expensive; they are also intended to last a long time. So, before you make a costly mistake, consider these points:

- Do you need a sleep sofa? They're usually more expensive than and not as comfortable as other sofas, so buy one only if you need a place for frequent sleepover guests. (An inflatable bed is a good alternative.)

- Do you already have upholstered chairs in the room? If so, buy a sofa whose back is the same height as, or within three to five inches of, those of the chairs. You'll avoid the unpleasant "roller-coaster effect" that is one of the ten most common decorating mistakes.
- How much "wear and tear" will your sofa have to withstand? Do you have young children? Pets? Do you eat on your sofa? For durability and easy care, choose a rayon chenille, corduroy, or tightly woven fabric in a medium-to-dark color. Ultrasuede HP (high performance) is another wonderful option. It comes in about fifty colors and can be easily cleaned with soap and water. Small, pin-dotted patterns also hide stains well. Leather, in a dark, neutral color (saddle, tobacco, cocoa, or black) works well in a family room or den, but fabric is still the best bet for most living rooms.
- How long will you be living in your present home? If you're planning to stay five years or more, you can tailor your needs to the current space and perhaps choose a large modular-seating unit for your family room. But if you think you might be moving, a bulky piece of that kind might not work in a smaller space.
- If you are considering a very large sofa, remember that it will have to fit through the doors and hallways when it's delivered—so measure carefully.

The Well-Made Sofa

Construction is the most important factor in determining both the durability and comfort of your sofa. So be sure you consider the following factors:

- The frame should be made of hardwood, not plywood or pine.
- Look for eight-way hand-tied springs. Those that provide each of the seat cushions with its own suspension deck are best. Curved or modular seating sometimes does not allow for this kind of construction and uses webbing instead.
- Buy the best quality fabric you can afford, and if it is patterned, be sure the seams are straight and the pattern matches where it joins.

- Cushions stuffed with a combination of down and feathers wrapped over foam or springs are softer than poly/Dacron cushions and require less maintenance than those stuffed with down alone.
- Be sure that none of the back or seat cushions are sewn down, so that they can be rotated, since turning the cushions will add years to the life of your sofa.

Sofa Style

Sofas, like everything else, come in several styles. The ones listed below are basic, and knowing what they're called will help you to communicate what you want. Conventional sofas are generally from eighty to ninety-three inches long. Any of the styles described here can also be found in loveseat size, which is from sixty to seventy-five inches.

SLIM-ARM SOFA has straight, thin, medium-to-high arms. There are either two or three cushions on both the seat and the back. Not as comfortable for "nappers" as either the Tuxedo- or Lawson-style sofas. This style is best suited to modern or eclectic rooms.

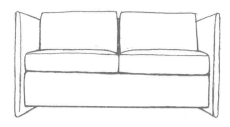

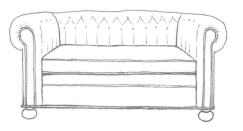

CHESTERFIELD: This is a completely tufted sofa with high, rolled arms and a tight seat that does not have a cushion. Usually upholstered in leather, it is a classic that can be used in any style home.

LAWSON has either large or small rounded arms. There are usually three cushions on the back and on the seat, but some may also come with two larger ones. This style works in both traditional and eclectic rooms.

TUXEDO has straight, square, low-to-medium-height arms. There are usually three cushions on the seat and three on the back. This is a classic sofa that works in both traditional and modern rooms.

FLAIR-ARM SOFA: The arms are similar to those of the slim-arm sofa but are attached at an angle to the seat. This style usually has either one or two seat cushions and a "tight" back, meaning that there are no cushions on the back. It works with either eclectic or modern-style rooms.

CAMELBACK: The distinctive "hump" in the middle of its back gives this classic its name. Its curvy Victorian lines and, in many cases, wooden rather than upholstered arms are best suited to a country-style or antique-filled room.

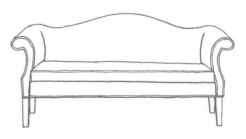

Remodel Your Modular Furniture

You might be moving to a smaller space or simply have grown tired of the look. In either case, you can use what you have but give it an entirely different feeling by taking your modular sofa apart and turning it into a more conventional sofa (by using two corner sections and one armless section) and two slipper chairs (two separate armless sections).

Plump Those Pillows

If your sofa has lost its oomph, you don't necessarily have to replace it. Instead, consider having the seat and back cushions restuffed with Dacron or a combination of Dacron and down. If the fabric is worn, remove the old fabric, cover the cushions in muslin, and then have custom slipcovers made. This option will cost half as much as reupholstering, and the slipcovers can be removed for easy cleaning.

Long Live the Cushions

To keep upholstered seating looking fresh and feeling firm, do what the professionals do: Turn over every seat *and* back cushion several times a week. And, if your sofa has loose back cushions, take it a step further and switch the left one with the right when you flip them, especially if they come out over the sofa arms. (This is called a T cushion.) You'll notice the difference immediately, and your cushions will last a lot longer.

Reminder: Avoid purchasing any chair or sofa that has its cushions sewn on so they can't be turned.

Pattern, Pattern Everywhere

Multiple patterns may look great in decorating magazines, but they may also be visually chaotic and, therefore, hard to live with unless you have a very large space. For a coordinated and tranquil room, stick to only one busy pattern (if any), and use these simple guidelines:

- If you already have one item, be it a rug, a sofa, or a pair of chairs, with a busy pattern, all the other elements in the room should be simple.
- To coordinate with a pattern, choose contrasting solids, stripes, or pin dots.
- If your chairs are upholstered in a pattern, choose a solid for the sofa. If your chairs are solid, then your sofa might well be your one patterned piece.
- Use patterns that are appropriate to the size of the piece—large is okay for a sofa, but smaller and tighter are better for smaller side chairs.
- If you are a minimalist or a modernist who eschews pattern, you can use contrasting textures instead.
- Use contrasting welting to accent a solid upholstery fabric for a stylish, finished look.
- Use a couple of throw pillows in the same fabric as your chair as "accents" on your sofa. 18" pillows work well for sofas, while 14" to 16" pillows are the right scale for loveseats.

A Simple Sofa Makeover

Tired of your tailored, Lawson-style sofa? Give it an entirely new look simply by adding a four-inch-long fringe all around the bottom. An upholsterer can do the job, or you can purchase a special rounded needle and sew it on yourself.

Making the Most of a Small Space

Is your entrance foyer or vestibule too small to accommodate a commode or table? Try a narrow bench instead. It will be handy for setting down packages and sitting on to remove wet boots. These benches come in a variety of styles, from plain wood to partially or completely upholstered to those with cane seats. (See Resources.)

Through the Looking Glass

If you have a glass-topped coffee or dining-room table and are tired of keeping Windex in business, replace the top with marble, granite, distressed wood, or even metal, depending on the style and color of your room.

Out of Love with Your Loveseat?

I'd love to meet the person who came up with the idea of selling a matching loveseat-and-sofa combination. What a clever way to sell an extra piece of furniture by convincing the innocent buyer it would be an easy way to provide additional seating. Great marketing, yes. More seating, yes. And also the most uncomfortable configuration there is.

My company's Web site, redecorate.com, has a message board, and almost every day we hear from someone who is pulling her hair out trying to make her loveseat/sofa combo work. Here's the deal: There are only two viable situations for loveseats:

1. If you have a small living room or family room with a fireplace centered on one wall, you can have a *pair* of loveseats facing each other across a rectangular coffee table, perpendicular to the fireplace.

2. If you have a large, wide room, a loveseat-and-sofa L-shaped combination can be turned into a U-shaped configuration with the addition of a pair of matching chairs across from the love seat.

In almost every other case, a loveseat creates problems and is best replaced by a pair of chairs. The chairs are more adaptable to small spaces and allow for intimate conversation between two people facing one another—the ideal way to chat.

Make It More Practical

Do your end tables have drawers or closed storage shelves and unfinished backs? If they are wide, you can save space by turning them so that the backs face the sides of your sofa. The tables will look cleaner and less bulky, especially in a small room.

Sturdy Surfaces

Wherever you sit in a living room, family room, or den, a place to set things down—a coffee table, end tables, or their equivalent—should be within easy reach. It's 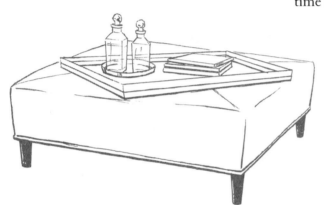 time for an adjustment if you must lift your bottom off the seat in order to reach a table. Here are some ideas to inspire you to use what you have and to make you and your guests most comfortable:

- Use an ottoman as a coffee table, but be sure to set a large, sturdy metal or wooden tray on top for holding glasses or other items that might otherwise topple over.
- In addition to storage space, a flat-topped trunk provides a large surface upon which to rest books, magazine, and snacks.
- For additional resting space, use a small, low bureau or commode as an end table.
- Stacking tables come in handy for casual meals in the family room, or to provide places for chips or drinks.
- If there's not enough room for a regular coffee table in your living room, you can use a matching pair of porcelain Chinese garden seats instead. Usually thirteen inches in diameter, these will give you a large enough surface for a glass or a book. A pair of them, which can be easily moved, will provide two or more people with places to rest things.

How to Teach an Old Desk New Tricks

An old, small, wooden desk with a kneehole opening and two or three drawers on either side can be turned into a lovely dressing table. Refinish or paint the piece if necessary, and add a new marble or glass top. A small stool on wheels can be tucked underneath. Place a pedestal-style makeup mirror (with magnification on one side) in the middle of the vanity. Use an attractive tray in silver, brass, or wood to display perfume bottles, and complete the look with a framed photo in the same finish as the tray.

Glass Gallery

If the surface of your desk or bureau is scratched, instead of refinishing the whole piece, you can have a piece of glass cut to fit the top. The glass alone will hide scratches, but if you slip photos underneath it you will also create a display that requires no upkeep and takes up no space.

Seating Solutions

- In small rooms, use armless upholstered chairs such as "slipper" style, which will allow more space than chairs with arms but will provide a more comfortable, small-scale alternative to wooden chairs.

- If you have both a television and a fireplace in your living room or family room, make it easy to watch TV and at the same time enjoy a nice view of your roaring fire by using swivel chairs that allow both movement and flexibility.

- If your budget won't allow you to buy a pair of matching chairs, purchase one chair and a matching ottoman. Until you can afford the second chair, use the ottoman as a "second" seat by placing the chair on one side of your coffee table and the ottoman on the other side. You'll have two places to sit with the effect of a matching pair.

Flexible Furnishings

A yoga teacher who lived and worked in a very small house in the suburbs called for a consultation on her living room, a narrow, ten-by-thirteen-foot sunny space that held only a sofa, a rectangular, pointy, glass-topped coffee table, and a cart for the television and audio equipment.

The woman explained that she found the space awkward both for entertaining and for giving private classes. Since the sofa was the only seating in the room, she and her visitor had to sit side by side and were forced to twist their bodies in order to face each other when chatting. When I'm talking with friends socially, I want to face them comfortably without having to rotate my body. And besides that, the sofa and heavy coffee table are in my way when I want to use the living room for classes. It doesn't feel peaceful."

In the adjoining sunroom, I noticed a small, modular sofa consisting of four armless seats, which were lined up in a row, sofa style. I asked if we could possibly switch the seating in the two rooms, and she agreed. We moved the sofa into the sunroom and the modular seating into the living room. In the center of the living room, we separated the sectional pieces and arranged the four in a circle around a small, round, low, wooden pedestal table I had found in her bedroom.

Suddenly, the whole room looked and felt different. No matter where one sat, it was easy to see the other person (or people) without difficulty, and more people could now be seated in the room.

I suggested that she add casters to the armless seats since they were low to begin with and the wheels would also give her flexibility when she wanted to clear the floor for a yoga session. The round, wooden table was light and easy to move, as was her TV cart.

When we'd completed the new arrangement, she looked very happy and said, "Now my living room is flexible, just like me!"

The Place for Space

When you walk around your home, are you comfortable, or do you feel as if you were navigating an obstacle course? If your furniture is creating obstacles to your comfort, here are a couple of problem areas to watch out for:

- Be sure your living-room chairs and sofa are grouped close together. Otherwise, anyone walking through the room will be forced to cross between those who are seated and interrupt their conversation.
- If possible, avoid having the traffic pattern cross in front of the television. To keep from blocking anyone's view, try to reconfigure the seating so that someone "passing through" will be walking behind the sofa instead of in front of it.

Bigger Is Not Always Better

Few of us have dining rooms/areas that are large enough to accommodate a full-size table with all the leaves in place and all the chairs around it—and still have any walking space left. Unless you have a very large family and need to seat six to eight people on a daily basis, remove the leaves from your dining-room table so that you have extra space when you're not entertaining.

A round pedestal table with one or two leaves stored in its base is the perfect choice for a small dining room. (See Resources.)

You might also consider "lending" the host and hostess armchairs to another room rather than leaving them at either end of a sideboard or china cabinet as most people are inclined to do. Try slipcovering them and using them in your entrance foyer, flanking a console or commode. Or perhaps you can use one or both of them in your bedroom(s). When there's company for dinner, simply remove the slipcovers and, *voilà!* you can instantly reunite your set.

If you're in the market for a new set of dining-room chairs, buy only the armless style so that you can seat more people more comfortably.

Wheeler Dealer

When it comes to interior design, flexibility is always a good thing. To that end, adding casters or wheels to certain furnishings will enhance their functionality.

Wouldn't it be easier to use that small, pull-up chair in your living room if it had little brass casters on it? Ottomans can also benefit from added wheels, as can certain coffee tables and even dining-room chairs. And if your dining-room table or chairs are too low, adding those wheels will solve your problem.

Something Old, Something New

If you purchase or inherit an old piece of furniture that is not valuable and decide to paint it, consider retaining the original hardware. Antique polished brass, copper, or steel handles or knobs will give the newly painted piece a more interesting look than new, updated hardware, and will help to maintain its original integrity.

Tale of a Hardware Transformation

One of my clients had an oak, five-drawer dresser that was the perfect size for her small bedroom. The piece suited her storage needs, and she liked its simple lines, but she was tired of its turn-of-the-century, Victorian hardware. We checked to see if the ornate pulls could be removed without damaging the wood. They could, and we realized once they were gone that the whole look of the chest had changed. The following week, my client found several bronze, Asian-style handles that coordinated with several bronze Japanese accessories she already had in her room. With this small change, the chest was transformed to highlight the Asian aesthetic she preferred.

To Stain or Not to Stain . . .

What do you do with an inherited piece that doesn't match the wood finishes in your home? There are two choices:

If the piece is valuable and, therefore, should not be refinished, try to find an isolated spot for it—perhaps in an entrance foyer, an upstairs hallway, or a guest room—where there are no clashing wood pieces nearby.

If refinishing is an option, you can easily change the stain to integrate the heirloom with your other furnishings and enjoy it.

Customized Marble

Any old bureau, commode, or Bombé chest can be refinished if its top is scratched. But if it's in a high-traffic area where chances are it will be damaged again, consider replacing the existing wood top with a piece of marble that has been sealed to prevent staining. Practical, strong, and elegant, marble can be cut to size and comes in many colors. Check with your local marble yard for prices and available stock.

One Plus One Equals ONE

Place two identical, small, square or flat-sided cabinets side by side and add a marble top to create a server for your dining room or an entrance piece for your foyer.

In the Land of Giants

Too many tall pieces in one room can be overwhelming.

If, for example, you have a large wall unit on one wall, do not put additional tall bookcases on other walls in the same room. Too many tall pieces will dwarf the lower furnishings and make the room visually uncomfortable. Conversely, a single tall piece should be balanced by placing a potted tree or a large painting on the opposite wall.

Use What You Need

A couple in their late forties had both lost their parents within a very short period of time and inherited furnishings from two homes—at least one more houseful than they needed or could use. Although they had donated many items to charity, they still found themselves left with a lot of furniture and artwork they didn't know what to do with. Their own furniture was an eclectic mix and they tried to incorporate as many of their parents' pieces as they could, but no matter what they did, their home still looked like a furniture warehouse. So they called my firm for help.

When I arrived and saw the pieces lined up, virtually one next to the other, I knew that many of their inherited treasures would have to go. But I also realized there was something much more important than furniture at issue here. Both these people felt compelled to hang on to their parents' gifts even though they didn't need many of them, simply out of guilt.

We talked about their feelings, and when they realized how many of their contemporaries were dealing with the very same problem, they became more comfortable deciding which pieces might really be useful to them and which were just taking up space.

We were careful to ensure that both sides of the family were represented as we determined what would be kept—a desk and buffet from hers, a beautiful mahogany bedroom set from his—and what would be given away or sold.

Instead of letting sentiment and guilt get in the way of practical decision-making, they were able to genuinely cherish each piece they kept, not only because it had belonged to their loved ones but also because it was enhancing their home and serving a real function.

Match Your Metals

Select like metal elements in your furnishings to establish which alloy should be used throughout the room. If your sofa has steel legs, use steel lamps and picture frames to give the space a pulled-together look. If most of your artwork is framed in gold leaf, use brass lamps and accessories.

Piano Arrangements

If you're cramped for space, place your baby grand or grand piano with its straight side parallel to the wall. If you have plenty of room, on the other hand, place it so that the person playing will be facing the conversation area of the room.

Matching the Mix

Do you have a piano with an unmatched bench? Here are a few ways to be sure they play beautiful music together:

- If the piano is stained ebony, simply paint the bench a semigloss black.
- If the bench is wood, refinish it to match the stain of the piano, or faux paint it in brown "wood" tones that coordinate with the wood of the piano.
- Reupholster the entire bench and use the same fabric as an accent on throw pillows for the sofa.

Bedside Storage

Bedside tables with two good-sized drawers, which provide storage for socks and underwear, are a practical alternative to slender-legged tables with little or no closed storage space whose beauty is only skin deep.

Spatial Relations

To create the illusion of open space as you enter the bedroom, place your bed on the wall opposite the doorway. If you can't manage that arrangement, try to place it as far from the doorway as possible in order to maintain an open traffic pattern.

Don't Go Off the Deep End

If your bedroom does not have sufficient space for a standard headboard *and* footboard, use *only* a shallow, flat headboard. Although many wooden headboards might *seem* shallow, they are often curved in such a way that they can take up ten to twenty inches of precious space. (See Resources.)

Pillow Talk

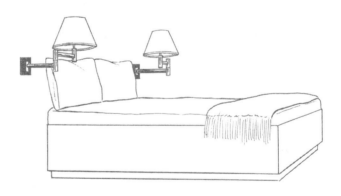

Don't have the budget or space for a decorative headboard? Create an oasis of calm and define the focal point of the room by using square European pillows (one for a twin-, two for a queen-, and three for a king-size bed) covered with matching shams and set upright against the wall at the head of the bed. Flank the bed with matching swing-arm lamps, and complete the new look with a pair of framed prints or one large painting centered five or six inches above the pillows.

All Things Not Being Equal

If you don't have an equal amount of space on either side of your bed and have to use bedside tables of different sizes, make sure they are at least the same height and in the same wood finish to give the room a more uniform look.

If you are making do with a small end table on one side that doesn't match the wood stain of the larger piece, drape the small table in a solid-color fabric that complements the wood of the larger piece to fool the eye and make the discrepancy less conspicuous.

Moving Madness

A Canadian couple had moved from a house in Ontario to an apartment in Manhattan. Although they'd certainly thought about which pieces of furniture to take and which they would have to leave behind, when they started arranging what they'd brought they became totally confused and called me in to "straighten them out."

As we tackled each room in turn, my clients were amazed to discover that the pieces they'd assumed would be perfect in one place turned out to be much more appropriate in another.

We created a work space in the formal dining room by bringing in a desk from the master bedroom. When covered with a tablecloth, it would also double as a server. A Japanese screen from the living room was turned into a beautiful headboard, and so it went.

By the time we were done, the couple was not only happily surprised by the results but also thrilled to have saved a significant amount of money.

Avoiding Must-Have Mistakes

It always surprises me that so many people place their furnishings in rooms where they don't use them or where the pieces themselves are inappropriate. Desks stand unused in hallways, bookcases inhabit dining rooms where they serve no purpose, and benches are stuck in the corners of family rooms where a recliner would be much more useful. The paradox is that very often these pieces would be extremely useful—and would look much better—if they were moved to another location.

Sometimes the problem arises because people see something they like and simply "must have" it. They buy a piece of furniture on impulse only to discover, once it has been delivered to their home, that it doesn't fit the space for which it was intended. Or they buy a piece they "love," thinking they'll figure out where to put it once they get it home, and then find that it doesn't work anywhere. That leaves lots of unhappy people who have wasted money, or who have furniture they like but cannot find a home for, or who don't know how to make their new pieces work with what they already have. That's when they call me.

Before they make another mistake by giving away something they really love, I help them find the best configuration for their pesky pieces—and in many instances, the ideal placement is in a location they would never have considered.

So, before you run out to buy something you think you need, look around the house and analyze what is there. You may already have what you need. And because I want to make sure you will not make any expensive, aggravating mistakes, here are the basic "must haves" for each room in your home:

Entrance Foyer
- Commode with drawers or closed storage OR, if your space is very small, a shelf
- One or two chairs OR, if space is limited, a bench

Living Room
- One sofa with two upholstered chairs OR two upholstered loveseats with two chairs (upholstered or not)
- A coffee table

- Two lamps—floor or table models
- Two end tables (if you have chosen table lamps)
- One area rug (6' x 9' to 9' x 12') OR carpeting

Bedroom
- Bed (headboard and footboard optional)
- Two bedside tables with closed storage, if space allows
- One bureau and/or one chest, depending on the available space
- Carpeting OR a pair of bedside runners
- A pair of lamps, either swing-arm style or table models

Family room
- Sofa
- Two chairs
- Entertainment center OR wall unit that incorporates all audio/video equipment, bookshelves, and closed storage
- A pair of pharmacy or table lamps
- A trunk OR a coffee table with a shelf
- Wall-to-wall carpeting OR an area rug

Dining Room
- To avoid pointy corners, I suggest a round, oblong, or oval dining table, preferably on a pedestal to save space.
- Four to eight armless dining chairs, all wood, all upholstered or with upholstered seats and/or backs
- A buffet with closed storage (if space allows)

Guest Room

- Two twin beds OR one full- or queen-size bed OR a sleep sofa
- One or two bedside tables
- One bureau with four to six drawers (this can be used in between two twin beds in place of bedside tables if space is limited)
- One or two table or swing-arm lamps
- Carpeting OR wood floor (small rug optional)

Study/Guest Room

- Desk with computer station, room for office equipment, and an open area for writing (this can be incorporated into a wall-to-wall bookcase or a closed wall unit with storage)
- Sleep sofa with queen-size bed
- Desk chair on wheels
- One or two end tables with lamps OR two standing lamps and one desk lamp

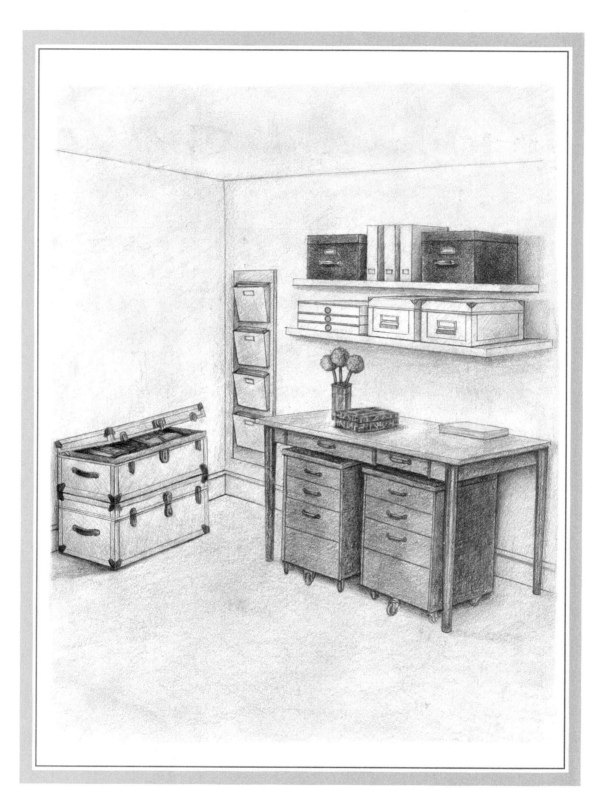

CHAPTER 3

Finding a Place
for Everything

No matter where you live, there never seems to be enough room for storage. No matter how large your home, your belongings always seem to expand to overflow the space.

Just in the last decade, we have seen a proliferation of shops and catalogs that specialize in helping consumers find clever ways to store their stuff. For a price, mini-storage warehouses are now providing apartment dwellers with the equivalent of a basement or attic.

The biggest issue for most people is finding sufficient *closed* storage. Open shelving, wall units composed mostly of display space, and end tables without drawers or doors do nothing to alleviate the problem of clutter.

It's no longer just the pack rats, hoarders, and compulsive collectors who need space salvation: growing families, entrepreneurs with home offices, and folks who inherit cherished family heirlooms are all engaged in the perpetual pursuit of new ways to organize and store their belongings. In order to make our homes feel tranquil, we must combat visual chaos.

Use It or Lose It

The best way to create more storage space is to clean out your clothes closet, and yet that seems to be the hardest thing for many people to do. Here are my personal tips for successful closet cleaning:

1. Remove everything and lay it on the bed, divided into categories: sweaters, blouses, slacks, etc.

2. Set up three big boxes or plastic bags: one for charity; one for things to be thrown away; one for items to go to the cleaner or laundry.

3. Anything that you haven't worn in a year, that is no longer in style, or that isn't in good condition *does not go back in the closet.*

4. Group slacks, blouses, skirts, and sweaters according to color and season. Out-of-season clothing goes in the back of the closet, leaving room for what you're wearing *now* in front. Grouping items by color makes it easier to find tops and bottoms that go together.

5. Keep all long dresses together in one section of the closet.

6. Hang belts from hooks high up on the inside of the closet door. Hang shoe bags below.

7. Keep like foldable items together, either on shelves or in dresser drawers.

Once you've finished "cleaning out," you might want to invest in some closet organizers, such as accessory bags, stacking storage boxes, hanging shelves, or over-the-door shoe holders, to help you keep things under control. (See Resources.)

The Dynamic Duo

Like love and marriage, sleep sofas and trunks used as coffee tables are a natural combination. A flat-top trunk will hold guest linens and blankets. (You might also consider adding casters to the trunk so that it rolls away easily when you want to open the sofa bed.)

Stylish Stackables

Stack two or three small antique suitcases or trunks one on top of another, and use them in the bedroom both for storage and as a bedside table to support a phone and clock radio, or as a side table next to a chair in the living room.

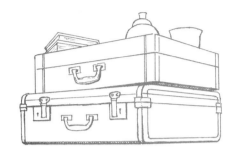

Videos Need Not Be on View

Be sure that your television is housed in or sitting on a piece of furniture that has drawers or a closed cabinet where your videos and tapes can be stored out of sight. There's no need to keep a stack of videos on view when you are not watching a movie.

Towering Discs and Toppling Tapes

Towering CD units may hold some of your favorite music but are not always the best solution, aesthetically or functionally, especially for formal rooms. Instead of taking up valuable floor space, house your CDs in a cabinet with shallow drawers, which are ideal for storing them out of sight. Drawers usually provide more storage space as well.

That's Entertainment

One way to store CDs, tapes, and a lot of other things is in an entertainment unit. Many people don't realize how useful these units can be for storing items that aren't necessarily intended for "entertainment."

Most ready-made units provide lots of open shelving but not much closed storage. That's fine if you have only books and family photos you'd like to display. But if you need space for items you'd rather not keep on view—files, extra candles, silver, even table linens, vases, wine and liquors, or glassware, you might want to consider having a unit custom-made to suit your particular needs. You'll be able to keep all these things, as well as your television, VCR, CD player, tapes, and CDs behind closed doors yet easily accessible. And if you're having the unit built, make sure the section for the TV is equipped with pocket doors and a pullout swivel shelf.

Good News for Newspapers

The best solution for storing old newspapers is to read them and "store" them in the trash, but if you must hold on to them, a covered basket will conceal your "stash" and keep things looking neat.

Read What You Have

Do you have more magazines than your magazine rack can hold? Here is one way to keep a lot of periodicals tidy and visible, so that you don't forget to read them.

Get three or four Lucite magazine holders, turn them horizontally on their sides with the openings facing out, and stack them against the wall, one on top of another. Arrange all the bindings of the magazines facing out so that you can read the titles easily. This arrangement can be tucked into a corner or stacked on a table and it will not take up a lot of space, while allowing you to see what you have.

Seek and You Shall Find . . . More Storage Space

If you are looking for more storage space, consider *any* open space from floor to ceiling. Under that leggy Parsons table there's space for a small antique trunk or a decorative box. Above a console or sideboard, there's wall space for a closed, hanging, wooden cabinet; on either side of a heating/air-conditioning unit there's room for built-in cabinets. Whatever you choose, closed storage is better than open shelving unless you want to display the items being stored.

See What You've Got

Sliding closet doors allow you to view only half the contents at a time. Replace those sliders with two standard or bi-fold wooden doors that open out from the center and allow you to see everything that is inside at once. Or install French doors with small panes of frosted or mirrored glass. To complete the look, add beautiful doorknobs or handles that coordinate with the other metal finishes in the room.

Dresser Decor

Bedroom bureaus with lots of little bitty accessories on top tend to make the whole room feel chaotic.

Replace several small keepsake boxes with one big beautiful box in wood, metal, or leather for storing small objects. Display a beautiful silver or brass tray, and add fresh flowers or a framed photo to complete the tabletop tableau.

No Butler? Get a Valet Instead

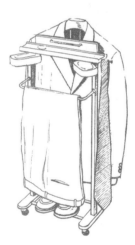

In an ideal world, all men would be neat and tidy and would not leave their clothing lying around. But if your man leaves his clothing on the bed instead of hanging it in the closet, and his change and wallet on top of your bureau, place a wood-and-brass valet in the corner of your bedroom. I guarantee that, as if by magic, he will begin to hang his clothing on it. If your partner is good about hanging his suit in the closet, give him a nice leather box, or a tray, or even a decorative plate where he can put small items neatly on the top of his bureau.

Vanity, Vanity

You can have the luxury of a dressing table to put on makeup and create extra storage as well, all without buying an extra piece of furniture for the bedroom. Here's how: Use the empty space under the window to build a wall-to-wall storage unit and simply paint it the same semigloss color as the wood trim in your room. Allow space for a kneehole opening where you sit, and build drawers on either side for storage. Make sure there's an outlet nearby for plugging in a hair dryer or a lighted mirror. Display pretty perfume bottles or attractive containers for cotton balls and other necessities on a tray.

The Jewels in the Crown

In the past, women traditionally kept their jewelry in large, specially made leather boxes with velvet linings and pullout compartments. Today, it's difficult to find such cases (and when you *do* find one, it's expensive), so baubles and bangles tend to be stored in various places throughout the bedroom. Here are a few suggestions for ways to organize jewelry so that it is easy to find when you want it:

- A hatbox displayed on the bureau, with homemade cardboard dividers to separate necklaces, earrings, bracelets, and rings
- A department store gift box sprayed with textured paint or covered with a fabric that matches the décor of your room
- A decorative, hinged wooden box that is both attractive and functional
- Corkboard hung on the inside of a closet door with pushpins to hang necklaces, pins, or pouches holding other baubles
- Display pins that aren't too heavy by hanging a plain white T-shirt on a hanger and pinning the pins to the shirt. Hang the shirt in the closet, where your pins will be handy when it is time to get dressed.

The Bed in the Wall

If you order a Murphy bed, be sure there are side shelves incorporated into the design. The narrow shelf that is usually provided behind the mattress is too small to hold bedroom basics such as a clock radio and a telephone.

Finding a Solution for the Spatially Challenged

A woman with whom I had worked several times called again after moving into a new home.

She had purchased an armoire for her dining room because she needed a lot of storage space for her china and silver, but as soon as she started unpacking, she realized the piece would not hold as much as she had thought. She had spent a lot of money and now, not only did she still not have the storage space she needed, but she also wasn't quite sure what to do with the armoire.

When she showed me into the dining room, the first thing I noticed was a twenty-foot-long wall with several large windows going almost all the way across it. And the window wall was actually recessed from the two adjacent walls by two feet. There lay the solution.

I suggested that she have a built-in storage unit made to fit the entire recessed area under the windows. Not only would this give her a great deal of closed storage space, but with the addition of a limestone top, she could also use the entire twenty-foot length as a server for buffet dinners.

With the storage problem solved, we were left with the issue of what to do with the armoire.

As it turned out, her teenaged daughter's bedroom furniture had the same bleached wood finish as the armoire, and she needed more storage space for sweaters and other foldable clothing.

Are Your Linens Near Your Laundry?

Some home builders put the linen closet on the second floor and the laundry area on the first, which requires unnecessary legwork. Having your linen closet next to or near your laundry area saves both time and steps. If there isn't one nearby, an armoire, or even a portable canvas closet, will do the trick. (See Resources.) Just try to keep a few extra towels in the bathroom for emergencies, and you'll be all set.

Recycled Storage

When your child outgrows his or her "baby" dresser or chest, move it to the garage for storing tools and supplies.

The small drawers are ideal for storing screws, nails, and all the sundry little things that one needs for do-it-yourself projects.

Hooked on Space

To create more space in your entry hall, replace the traditional standing coatrack with individual brass or steel coat hooks mounted randomly on the wall or in one or two straight rows.

CHAPTER 4

Windows to the World

Our windows are our connection to the world. They allow us to have light, to see our surroundings, and to view the sky. With or without a great view, I like to think of windows as living art.

Until the second half of the twentieth century, there were very few window treatments to choose from. Most homes had simple curtains—sheers in the summer to let in the breeze on a warm day and heavily lined drapes in the winter to block drafts on cold nights. Wooden shutters with tiny louvers were popular for some private houses, especially city brownstones, and white metal venetian blinds gained favor in the 1950s and '60s.

By the 1970s, residential designers began to use vertical blinds, which had traditionally been found only in offices, mainly because their plasticized or metal vanes required little upkeep. Today, although we continue to use many of these treatments, there are many new, simple, yet elegant, options that require less maintenance than ever before.

Treat Your Elements Alike

If you choose a fabric window treatment, be sure to use the same material on one or more elements in the room—to cover a chair or sofa, for throw pillows, or even as a dining-room tablecloth or a dust ruffle on the bed.

Keep Your Options Open

If you love the look of antique stained-glass windows, you'd be wise to keep the resale value of your home in mind before making *permanent* changes to the exterior glass. Instead of replacing the clear glass, hang stained-glass panes from two S hooks suspended in front of your standard windows. You'll be able to enjoy the colorful glass while you live in the house, you'll be able to take it with you when you move, and the future owners will have the freedom to choose their own options.

Fooling the Eye

If you have a window with only a tiny bit of wall space on one side and a lot more on the other, try disguising the discrepancy by using a treatment that can be mounted on the inside of the window frame. This will allow the eye to focus on the window rather than the walls. Another option would be to swag a curtain in the direction of the wider wall and have it drape down on that side.

Curtain Call

Think practically when replacing your curtains. If your bedroom is drafty, consider using heavy, solid-color velvet or wool that will help block the chilly air. Make the curtains reversible by lining them with the same color linen or cotton as the heavy fabric. Show the "cooler" cotton or linen side in warmer weather and the heavier velvet side in the winter.

Dimming the Light from Above

Skylights are great for letting more light and sky into dark rooms, but many times those ceiling windows are in the wrong rooms and in the wrong places.

One client who had recently purchased a home with a large skylight in the middle of her bedroom was awakened every morning at five when the sun came up. A few months after moving in, she couldn't take the sleep deprivation any longer, so she rigged up a heavy velvet curtain that covered the opening and blocked all the light. It looked awful, and that's when she called me in.

Given the configuration of the room, it was impossible to move the bed out of the direct sun, so as an alternative to the velvet curtain, I suggested that an opaque pleated shade be set inside the frame of the skylight. This meant that the window would have to be covered all the time, but there was plenty of other light in the room from other windows. (Besides, the opaque shade would allow some diffuse light into the room.) In the end, however, once she pointed out that the window also leaked when it rained, I suggested that she might want to remove the skylight completely: an alternative she had apparently never considered.

The Well-Treated Window

Window treatments work well in only two lengths, those that hang to the windowsill and those that hang to the floor. Floor-length curtains look lovely if they're hung above the window frame from a pole with finials and curtain rings. If there's a built-in radiator or air conditioner under the window, keep the entire treatment inside the window frame, if possible, and no longer than the windowsill. Remember, no window treatment should ever end between the windowsill and floor.

Treat Your Sills Well

Windowsills can affect not only the appearance of your window treatments but also the appearance of the entire room. To enhance the look of your whole room:

- Keep sills fresh and clean by painting them with washable satin semigloss annually.
- If the sills are in poor condition, cover them with a piece of marble cut to fit. White Carrara marble is a good basic choice.
- Avoid using your windowsills to display knickknacks or photos. After all, you don't want to detract from the "living art" outside the window.

Made in the Shade

When deciding whether to get one or three shades to cover a triple window, consider function as well as aesthetics. Although one shade may look better, if you find that

you open and close the side windows, but not the center one, three separate shades will give you more flexibility. Or, if an air conditioner is set in one of the windows, separate shades will allow you to expose the AC in the summer but keep the remaining shades lowered to block the sun.

Putting the Top Down

An especially good window-shade choice is one that has "top-down" and "bottom-up" features. This allows for privacy when the shade covers the bottom of the window and still lets you see the trees and sky. With this kind of shade you can keep an air conditioner that's installed in the window covered when it is not in use, while allowing light in through the top half of the window. (See Resources.)

Keep it Simple

If your window frames are higher than your door frames, avoid swags or valences that will only add more height and thus accentuate the discrepancy. Opt instead for sheer or plain curtains or simple Roman or pleated shades set inside the window frame.

The Unpainted Truth

If you have stained or painted wooden shutters on your windows, consider having the molding and woodwork in the room stained or painted to match to give the room a cohesive look.

Climate Control

If you live in a climate that is warm most of the year, an air conditioner is a necessity. But if you use an air conditioner for only three months or so, consider getting a portable unit that can be removed from the window during the cooler seasons. You'll get more natural light, which is in short supply during the winter.

And, if your permanent AC allows drafts into the room, you can purchase an inexpensive padded air-conditioner cover.

Sit with Your Back to the Window

A wonderful view is always a plus, but most of the time the impact is greatest when you first walk into the room, or when you are standing up. Most views are difficult to see from a seated position, so don't arrange your sofa facing the window unless it is very low or you have a wall of sliding glass doors.

If you have at least two or three standard windows in a row or a large picture window with a beautiful view, make this the focal point of the room by placing your sofa with its back to the windows. Add a coffee table and a pair of chairs to complete the conversation area. There's a bonus, too, because you can hide an unsightly air-conditioning or heating unit behind the sofa.

Windows, Windows Everywhere

Builders and architects proudly erect homes with windows of different shapes, sizes, and arrangements, which means lots of decisions for you about which treatments to use. Here are a few of the most common "problem" windows and how to treat them:

1. Accent windows above standard or picture windows.

If you decide to use curtains on the lower windows, the upper windows should not be covered unless they are at least half the size of the lower windows. If you do cover them both, be sure they are covered with the same treatment. If too much sun is a problem, you can fit the upper window with a shade that is permanently drawn. In fact, pleated shades custom-made to fit both windows would be a simple solution for minimizing the disparity.

2. A semicircular (fan-light) window should be left bare or covered with a fan-shaped pleated shade.

3. A window closely flanked by a glass door.

Use the same treatment for both. One-inch wooden (not metal) blinds; Duette shades (see "Treatment Options," below); or gathered sheer curtains mounted inside the frame on rods top and bottom would all be good options.

4. Multiple windows of varying sizes on the same wall.

Keep it simple. The less elaborate the window treatment, the less obvious the discrepancies will be.

Mirror Images

"We love this view," said the couple who had just purchased a split-level suburban house. Indicating one of the two small windows in their L-shaped dining area, they pointed out how the sun, which was setting on the west side of the house, cast beams of warm golden light that reflected on the walls of the room.

"I just wish there were some way to see more of this view," said the husband.

When I suggested that the small wall on the opposite side of the dining room be mirrored in plain, clear-glass panels, running from floor to ceiling to reflect the panorama on the west wall, the couple balked.

"We're not the mirror type," said the husband. "We're into nature, not glitz."

"Let's go outside for a minute," I suggested, taking their stepladder with me. We walked around to the western side of the house and I opened the ladder. Pulling a mirror from my purse, I climbed up and asked the couple to step back and tell me what they saw in its reflection. "The sun and the trees," they both said.

"That is what you would see when you are in your dining room," I explained.

They looked at each other and smiled. The man laughed and said, "Did I say 'we're not the mirror type'? Who said that?"

Treatment Options

The heavy, lined draperies over sheer curtains that were almost de rigueur in the last generation are not as popular today. These days, simplicity has become the general rule of thumb. Here are a few simple, but elegant, options for a variety of situations:

1. *Silhouette* shades, made by Hunter Douglas, are an excellent choice when privacy and/or sunlight are at issue. These sheer shades have adjustable fabric vanes in the center that allow them to change from transparent to opaque. They can be made to fit either inside the window frame or just at the top of the outside window molding. Ele-

gant all on their own, they require no additional window treatment. They are also available in an opaque material for use in bedrooms.

2. Pleated shades, such as Hunter Douglas Duettes, that can be secured at both top and bottom are the best choice for tilt-and-turn windows. They are flat and won't fall forward when the window is tilted open.

3. Plantation Shutters, two to four inches wide, made of wood, and stained or painted, are a dramatic choice for dressing medium to large, and especially very tall windows. They work particularly well in traditional or modern rooms that require protection from the sun.

4. Two-inch-wide wooden blinds provide lots of style as well as light control and privacy. They are appropriate for any room of the house and are also available in both one-inch and three-inch widths.

Used either alone or in combination with curtains, wooden blinds can be made to coordinate with the finishes on your wood furniture. Or they can be stained with a color wash to complement the painted walls or trim. And the cotton tapes that hold the slats together can be color-coordinated with your upholstery.

5. Sheer curtains in white or ecru can be hung on tension rods inside the window frame or outside the frame on brackets or on poles with curtain rings. If they are hung outside the frame, they can be used in combination with either pleated or roller shades mounted inside the frame. This is a classic and cost-effective choice for almost any style home.

6. Fabric shades such as balloon shades work well in traditional-style homes and are especially appropriate in bedrooms. When made in a fabric that matches a bedspread or bed skirt, they provide an elegant custom look. Roman shades made in either a thin, gauzy linen or a heavier fabric always look clean and neat. They work well in any room in the house and with all decorative styles.

Solid Simplicity

If you have a patterned rug or upholstery, keep the curtains in that room a solid color that picks up one of the colors in the pattern.

Spray Wrinkles Away

Are you tired of having to iron those annoying wrinkles that always seem to find their way into your curtains and cotton or linen slipcovers? Spray them away with Wrinkle-Free Fabric Relaxant, which works on many rumpled fabrics. (See Resources.)

Plugging the Leaks

With heating costs on the rise, it's more important than ever to keep your home draft-free. If there are windows you absolutely *never* open in the winter, an insulator kit can help. It comes with a clear plastic sheet that can be applied around the inside of your window frame with tape and a hair dryer.

When the weather warms up, the covering can easily be removed without damaging either the frame or the window.

Creative Curtain Rods

If you're using traditional curtain rods, rings, or poles, be sure that the metal matches the other metals in the room.

If the windows in your den or child's bedroom are not too wide, you can use a piece of sports equipment in place of a metal pole to hang curtains. A golf club or hockey stick will highlight a window in a room with a sports-related theme.

In other rooms, a bamboo pole or even a dried tree branch will serve as a stylish curtain support.

If standard curtain rings do not fit on any of the above, use curtains that tie onto the pole. The ties are usually long enough to fit around the circumference of any decorative pole.

Creative Frosting

Many people think of frosted glass only as those wavy opaque panes that are found mainly in bathrooms. In fact, plain, smooth, frosted glass is a good choice for other rooms in your house, too.

A window in a narrow hallway that faces the house next door is a good candidate for plain, frosted glass because you won't need to clutter the hall with any other kind of window treatment. If your room overlooks a busy street, but you can see trees and the sky, opt for a double-hung window with frosted glass on the bottom for privacy and clear glass on the top for light and a view.

Clear as Glass

In addition to choosing the right coverings, it's important to keep the windows themselves looking their best. To keep them streak-free, wipe them with a Window Sparkle Cloth after you wash them to remove streaks, make the glass really shine, and help repel water the next time it rains. (See Resources.)

Staying Out of the Sun

Your window coverings can help to make your home more attractive in more ways than one. If no one is home during the day and both your dining room and living room get a lot of bright sunlight, save your fabrics and rugs from fading by closing the curtains or pulling down the blinds before you leave for work each morning.

CHAPTER 5

Illuminating Solutions

When you shop for lighting and are confronted with a seemingly infinite variety of fixtures and lamps, sconces and chandeliers, you may well be totally confused about which would be best for your particular needs. But remembering a few basic rules can go a long way toward dispelling the darkness and lighting up your life.

To start with, every room needs general, or overhead, lighting: recessed high hats, track lighting, chandeliers, or even torchère up-lights—anything, in fact, that provides light for the entire room emanating from the ceiling.

The next most important category of lighting for every room is task lighting. As the name implies, these are the lights you use to work, read, sew, or to do anything else that requires good, intense light focused on the work area: table lamps, pharmacy lamps, directional floor lamps, and kitchen counter lighting.

The third category is accent lighting, the only variety that is optional in residential design. Used for highlighting art, sculpture, and plants, these are the tiny pin-spot lights, painting lights, small up-lights, and sconces. Accent lights add drama and create an ambiance that neither general nor task lighting is able to do.

The kind of lighting you choose to fulfill each of these functions will have an impact on the aesthetics and comfort of every room in your home.

Coming Out of the Shadows

One of the most common lighting mistakes is also one of the most obvious. If you have a ceiling fixture that is lighting up your ceiling really well, it means that the rest of the room—the walls and the furnishings, not to mention the people—are cast in shadows.

Look at your ceiling. Is it brighter than anything else in your room? If so, it's time to correct your overhead lighting.

If you have a globe-shaped fixture or any type of up-light, you'll need to replace it with a down-light of some sort. A chandelier or track lighting that forces the light down to the floor would be the best choice both functionally and aesthetically. And by the way, today track lighting is being used in traditional-style homes too.

Don't Switch Tracks

If you install track lighting in more than one room of your home, use the same track fixture throughout for a cleaner, more cohesive look.

Stay Centered

Is your overhead lighting making your room feel off balance? Replace an off-centered ceiling fixture with L-shaped track lighting. This will allow you to direct the light to the middle of a dining-room table or to center the light in a foyer. Any room with off-center overhead lighting can benefit from switching to track lighting.

The Lowdown on Overhead Lighting

Standard eight-foot ceilings will appear higher if your overhead lighting fixtures are kept close to the ceiling. The chandelier over your dining table is one fixture that would not be hung close to the ceiling, but if your goal is to make the room appear more spacious, you would probably do best to stay away from this traditional form of lighting and stick with recessed or track lighting that hugs the ceiling.

You Can Take It with You

Although recessed lighting is functional and aesthetically pleasing, it may not always be the most practical or economical because most standard-height ceilings don't allow for easy installation. Particularly if you are a renter, install track lighting with several tiny halogen spotlights. This will allow you to direct the light where you need it without imposing on the space of the room—and you can take it with you when you move.

Halogen vs. Incandescent Lighting—Each in Its Place

Most recessed, track lighting, and torchères now have halogen bulbs. In fact, the advent of halogen lighting has had a tremendous impact on how we illuminate our homes. It provides full-spectrum light, which is whiter, brighter, purer, and shows truer colors while using less energy and, therefore, costing us less. But incandescent lighting still serves us well in sconces, table lamps, and chandeliers when we want a softer "glow."

The Angle on Lighting

If you have an angled or cathedral ceiling, install tiny, adjustable, recessed halogen lights inside black baffles (not white, chrome, or brass, which do not reduce glare as effectively) instead of big floodlights or "eyeball" lights that protrude from the fixture. The small spots will allow you to direct the light where you want it and will create much less glare than the larger incandescent fixtures.

An Illuminating Idea

If you have a lamp or chandelier with clear rather than frosted bulbs, it's time for a change. Those clear bulbs are casting harsh shadows on you and your room. Replace clear bulbs with frosted ones and purchase small clip-on shades to direct the light down, rather than up, onto the ceiling. Your rooms will look much better, and you'll no longer be straining your eyes.

Light Up Your Life

Whether you have seasonal affective disorder, live in Seattle, or work the late shift, a natural, full-spectrum light will make up for lost sunshine. (See Resources.)

Fixtures for Fixing Your Face

The ideal light for putting on makeup or shaving in your bathroom is lighting that runs down both sides of your mirror or medicine chest and does not cast shadows on your face as overhead lighting does.

If you must use an overhead fixture, be sure to put in frosted bulbs that cut down on glare.

Central Location

Many people mistakenly think their end tables and bedside tables will have more space for accessories and lamp cords will not show if the lamps are placed at the back of the tables, close to the wall. For a more balanced look, be sure to center the lamps on your tables. (Lamps on end and bedside tables should be in proportion to the table on which they stand, so you should have enough space to hold the essentials—a cup of coffee, a book, a clock—even when you place the lamp in the middle of the table. And resist cluttering up those end tables!)

The Lamps March Two by Two

Do you have an assortment of lamps in various shapes and sizes? First of all, eliminate odd lamps that are too big, too small, or the wrong style for the room. (Chances are, in the Use What You Have® tradition, that you'll find a place for these in other rooms!) Then, create harmony with matching pairs. Is there a tiny table lamp at one end of your sofa and a tall, standing lamp at the other end? Does the combination look off balance? Put the scale back in balance by keeping pairs together or acting as matchmaker yourself.

You can create that all-important "pair" by using two similar-size and -shaped lamps, crowned with matching shades. (New shades are a lot less expensive than new lamps.)

If you don't have room for two end tables, the next-best solution would be a pair of standing lamps set at either end of the sofa. But if you must use a table lamp at one end and a standing lamp at the other, you can still create the illusion of a "match" by making sure that both shades are the same distance from the floor.

Table-Lamp Tactics

Here are three rules to follow to get the most out of table-lamp lighting:

1. Use three-way bulbs in three-way lamps.
2. Use maximum wattage in all lamps.
3. Use white or ecru, linen or silk shades on lamps that are used for general illumination or reading. Paper shades, whether white or black, are opaque and do not provide sufficient light for a room or for doing tasks.

The Shade Is a Lamp's Crowning Glory

Here are some pointers for selecting the right shade for your lamp:

- If the lamp will be placed close to the wall, try using a simple rectangular shade or a rectangular pagoda-shaped shade.

- If the lamp will be placed on a round table, a round shade will mimic the shape of the table for a uniform look. Round "coolie hat" shades also spread the light at the widest possible angle, making for easier, more comfortable reading.
- Oval shades tend to look best on bedroom side tables and bureaus.
- Make sure that the shade covers both the harp and the lightbulb, but is not too big for the lamp.

The Finishing Touch

You can add an attractive accent by changing the finials that sit atop your lamps. These decorative fittings come in a variety of styles and finishes including metal, porcelain, glass, and wood. Finding the right one can bring just the right "extra something" to your table lamps.

Give Your Lighting a "Lift"

If you still have the round-knob type dimmer on your wall, it's time for an update.

The newer, vertical glider allows you to select the level of light you like best and leave it in that position while you use a button to turn the light on and off. In addition, the newer dimmers have a cleaner look and don't stick out from the wall as much as the older style does.

Stylish Switches

Although almost every room would benefit from a dimmer switch, you may still have switch plates. If so, be sure they are painted or wallpapered to blend with the color and covering of your walls. Use "cute," decorative, or color-contrasting switch plates in the children's room only.

CHAPTER 6

Decorating with Paint and Paper

The good news about paint is that it provides an easy way to dramatically change the look of a room. The bad news is that, in the wrong hands, this seemingly innocuous substance can wreak havoc with just a couple of coats.

What is it about choosing and using paint that makes it so tricky? It's like any new relationship. You bring it home and test it. It seems fine. You make the commitment and, *bam!* you find out you've made a big mistake—a big, expensive mistake. It's too pink! It's too dark! It's totally wrong!

So how do you avoid falling in love with the wrong paint while finding your true pigment? Look in the mirror and in your closet and get to know yourself first. Which colors do you wear often? Look around your house. Do you have a rug that will help you establish a color scheme? Remember that you'll be looking at this paint for a few years, so consider the long term. And here are a few other considerations: heavy traffic patterns, kids, pets, and the color schemes of the surrounding rooms.

Wallpaper is an even bigger commitment, both because it's usually more expensive than paint and because it's likely to be "hanging around" longer than your painted walls. But some people really love it, and, indeed, it can be beautiful. If you're one of those who can't resist its charms, just be sure to take the hints provided in this chapter that will keep you from wanting to tear it down, and from tearing your hair out as well.

Plan Before You Paint

Before you even venture into the paint store, there are a few questions you should be asking yourself:

- How much natural light does this room get? To maximize the light in a normally dark room, always paint the walls white. In a naturally bright room, you have more freedom to play with color, but it's still best to keep it light—a cream, light yellow, celery, or perhaps a very pale blue.
- How big is the room? The lighter the color, the larger and brighter the room will appear. If your room is naturally expansive and bright, you'll have more freedom in your choice of paint.
- Do I use the room during the day, when it's important to maximize the natural light, or will I be using it only in the evening, when brightness will come from artificial light? If you're using the room mainly at night, its natural "brightness" is less important, and you might consider a light neutral color for the walls rather than painting them white.
- What furniture is there now, or will there be in the room? Unless the walls are white, it's important to choose a color that coordinates well with the colors in your upholstery and carpet.

Raising the Ceiling with Paint

We all want high ceilings, and one way to achieve at least the feeling of height is to paint your ceilings white or the color of the walls if they are a creamy, neutral color. In fact, unless you are lucky enough to have ceilings with interesting moldings and architectural details that could be highlighted, there's no reason to draw the eye up by painting them anything *but* white. And remember that whatever color you use, unless your home is contemporary and your ceiling completely unblemished, you should always use flat paint on the ceiling.

Accentuate the Positive

When it's time to paint the interior of your home, remember to consider the architectural details. Many people automatically paint walls a color, then paint the trim white. But this technique is only effective when a room is symmetrical—windows all the same size and doors all the same height. Otherwise, think of the room as a "shell" and paint the walls and trim the same color for a more cohesive look.

My Biggest Blunder

My company's Web site, redecorate.com, runs a monthly contest in which visitors are asked to respond to a range of questions concerning their redecorating and design concerns. Once we posed the question "What was the biggest decorating blunder you have ever made?" The winning response came from a woman who, years ago, had painted her ceiling vivid red—while, as she confessed, "under the influence . . ."

Ceilings are, of course, usually best painted white or cream. Pastel colors work well, too, especially if the ceiling is higher than eight feet and in good condition. A light blue, soft yellow, or pale green can look pretty if the tint ties into a fabric or some other accent in the room.

So what happened to the woman with the red ceiling?

She stopped painting halfway through, and the next day was so appalled by what she'd done, she couldn't bring herself to finish the job. Less than a year later she moved out of the house, and a month or so after that, the house burned down. I guess it was bad karma.

Camouflaging with Color

Ever notice those annoying little jogs in the walls that prevent a room from being perfectly rectangular? Sometimes they are in the corners, but often you'll find them smack in the middle of a nice long wall. Wherever they are, they tend to make a room look choppy. To compensate for these "bumps" in the wall, and to give your room a more cohesive look, paint the whole room, including the ceiling, one color. This will help to camouflage the extraneous protrusion(s).

Harmony Throughout

If your home has an open floor plan, with no walls or doors between the "public" rooms such as the foyer, the living room, and the dining room, be sure to use the same paint for all the communal areas. Your space will look less chopped up and will appear larger.

If you want to make one particular area, such as the foyer, distinctive, use wallpaper in that one space and paint the remaining rooms one complementary color. If you would like to wallpaper the dining room, keep the foyer and living room the same color. But avoid papering only part of a wall, such as in a living/dining room combination, in an attempt to "define" the area. It will make it looked chopped up. (It is more effective to define the two areas with an area rug or the furnishings.)

The Doors in the Walls

Many people put a great deal of time and thought into choosing paint for their walls but leave the doors unpainted. Big mistake. Unless your home has beautiful carved wooden doors, paint them. Here's the secret: If all the doors in your house are the same size and style, you can paint them white or another accent color. If you have a variety of doors—sliders, standard, etc.—paint them all with semigloss paint in the same color as the walls of the room so that they are less obtrusive.

The same rule applies if you have two doors of different styles in one room. For example, if you have sliding glass doors with black metal frames on one side of a room and a standard wooden or pair of French doors painted white on the other side of the room, paint both the black metal and white French doors the same color as the walls to give the space a more pulled-together look.

A Serendipitous Mistake

A woman called our office in despair. She had painted her living room a rosy pink shade she thought would match her sofa fabric, but it looked too bright and garish on her walls. Even though she loved the idea of the pink, she knew she'd made a mistake.

When I saw the space, I had to agree that the pink paint was so flashy it made the whole room look bad.

The solution, however, turned out to be fairly simple. The room had lots of cream and off-white in the fabrics, paint trim, and lampshades, so I suggested that she add a color-wash treatment of cream and white on top of the pink to soften the harshness of the base color. After finding a book explaining the technique and all the necessary supplies in her local hardware store, the client decided she would attempt the project herself.

A week later she called to say it had all turned out to be a blessing in disguise. Her living room now looked beautiful, and she was so happy with the results that she was planning to use the same treatment in her bedroom, but with different, softer colors.

Which Paint Where

- Generally, it's best to use a flat finish on your ceiling as it hides imperfections and stays clean. The only exceptions are kitchens and bathrooms, where a semigloss is easier to maintain.

- Flat paint, which is difficult to clean, is best used in rooms whose walls have imperfections or where there isn't much traffic and most of the people who use the rooms are adults.
- Eggshell finish is somewhere between flat and semigloss. It has a slight sheen and can show some imperfections, but because it's easy to clean, it works well in high-traffic areas and in homes where there are children.
- Semigloss paint is always used for trim—including doors, windows, and baseboards, as well as bookcases, window seats, and radiator enclosures—no matter which finish is used on the walls, because it is the most durable and least vulnerable to dirt and wear.

Color Find

Are you confused about how to choose a new color scheme for one of the rooms in your home? When selecting paints and fabrics, it's best to work with just three to four colors total for the walls, furniture, and carpet. Keep in mind that your entire home will look better if at least two of these colors are carried into the other rooms as well. For example, if your living room is in a neutral palate of cream, taupe, and mushroom, you might carry two of those colors into another room and add an accent of ginger or black, creating a second palate of cream, taupe, and ginger or cream, taupe, and black. Here are three places you can look to find your new palette:

- Select colors from a patterned area rug.
- Choose colors from a patterned fabric.
- Use three or four colors from a large painting. Designate one dominant, one secondary, and one or two accent colors.

Color Coordination

Here's an inexpensive way to spruce up a ho-hum room. Whether you prefer a neutral or a bold color scheme, use one of the colors from your collection of accessories to give the space a pulled-together look. For example, a living room with white cotton duck slipcovers will look fresh and beautiful if one long wall is painted chartreuse and the same color is also reflected in several chartreuse-and-white striped throw pillows. You can also hang a group of green botanical prints in bamboo or gold-leaf frames on one wall. Place a couple of airy ferns in brass pots on the floor to reinforce the vibrant green color and complete the look.

Painting Brick
Thinking of painting a brick wall?

Although white is classic, you can actually make it any color you like, so long as you remember to use flat latex paint, which works best. And do bear in mind that you will not be able to remove the paint completely, so that you'll never again have the option of re-creating that pristine deep red brick. But the brick with a bit of the leftover white clinging to it can also be a pleasing, if different, look.

Blend in the Built-In
To save money and to help a custom-made built-in unit "disappear into the wall," have it made of an inexpensive wood such as pine, rather than a more expensive hardwood, then prime it and paint it the same color as the trim in the room. It will blend into the woodwork and make your room appear larger.

What Paper Where
Although I never recommend wallpaper for the living room unless you are looking for a cozy, Victorian, or "antiquey" feeling, virtually every other space in the house can be enhanced by wallpaper, so long as you use the proper paper in the proper place.

- Use vinyl paper only in bathrooms, kitchens, children's rooms, and heavily trafficked areas so that it can be easily wiped clean.
- The hallway or foyer is a perfect place for paper, but if there are children running up and down the stairs and dragging their sticky little fingers along the walls, make sure that the paper you use is vinyl here, too.

- Use "paper" wallpaper in more formal rooms or in spaces that don't receive much wear and tear.

Pattern vs. Texture

The secret to peace and harmony in the home is simplicity, and that goes for wallpaper, too. If you have a formal and traditional home, patterned wallpaper works well, so long as one of the colors in the pattern *exactly* matches one of the other colors in the room, and so long as there are no busy patterns in your upholstery fabrics or rugs. Pattern-on-pattern is a look that's hard to use successfully, so, when in doubt, keep it simple.

As an alternative to pattern, texture is the decorator's greatest ally, and there are now many textured papers that will provide a variety of interesting looks, from retro to modern, with no pattern at all.

The Faux Paint Alternative

Faux paint treatments, such as marbleizing, striating, or color-washing, can be a much less expensive way than hanging wallpaper to create interesting texture on your walls. Some of the larger paint stores even give classes in do-it-yourself texturizing with paint.

Grass Cloth Revival

Grass cloth is making a big comeback, and with good reason.

- It provides great texture without pattern.
- When you get tired of it, it can be painted, so that you can change your color scheme or the look of your room without having to remove it from the walls.

Making Sure It Sticks

If you're using a precoated wallpaper and want to be sure the seams don't separate, try adding extra adhesion such as Sure Grip® to prevent the seams from separating. (See Resources.)

Back to the Future with Paint

Just because you've chosen a bold or unusual color for one or more of your walls, don't think you have to live with it forever.

I recently worked with a woman whose large living room had one pale aqua wall that hadn't been painted in thirty years. To my knowledge, that's something of a record, and when I asked why she'd never repainted the wall, she told me this story:

She'd seen the color in a magazine in 1962. It was actually the color of an outfit worn by Jacqueline Kennedy. My client was just then moving into her apartment, and she liked the color so much that she'd cut out the article and asked the painter to match it. She then purchased fabric for her living-room chairs with the same aqua color in the pattern. Since then, she'd been reluctant to repaint because she was afraid the chairs would no longer match.

I first assured her that if she really wanted to keep the same color, she could take a chip from the wall to her local paint store and have it matched by computer. But I also suggested that it might be time for a change.

Her rug had a lovely pale salmon in the pattern, as well as a drop of the aqua, and a cream background. Perhaps she could paint the whole room salmon, which would still coordinate with both her rug and her chairs. For some reason, she'd never considered that alternative, and she was delighted with the change.

CHAPTER 7

The Bottom Line on Flooring

Floors demand attention. They take up a lot of space, help define the style of your home, and require regular maintenance. Your walls, whether they are painted or papered, require only minimum care, but the type of flooring you choose will determine the amount of time you spend taking care of it. And because flooring is neither easy nor inexpensive to change, you will probably be living with it a long time.

If you are like most people, you will consider changing a wood or tile floor only if you own your home and if the floor is either in very poor condition or in a style that you don't like. But whether you're an owner or a renter, if your floors are fairly neutral in style and in good shape, you will leave them intact. That doesn't mean there are no options for change, only certain parameters you probably should consider, such as which colors will "go with" the existing tile; which stains and protective coatings are best; and whether, where, and what kind of rug(s) or carpeting to use. The answers to these questions will be determined by your lifestyle—where you live, with whom you live, and how much time and energy you have to devote to your home.

Staining Strategies

Trying to decide what color to stain your wood floors? Look at all aspects of the room before making an expensive decision: furnishings, available light, size and proportions of the room, and your own decorating goals. The general rule would be to use a dark wood stain if most of your furniture and upholstery is dark. However, dark colors do tend to make spaces look smaller and light colors make them look bigger. So, in a small room that does not have much natural light, using a light pickled-wood floor even if the furniture is dark will make the space appear larger and lighter. To do this, all your wood furniture should be uniform in color and the walls should be light—white or beige. The look you achieve will be very dramatic.

If your upholstered furniture is done in light fabrics or your wooden pieces are stained in light tones, a light floor will give the room a breezy, open feeling while a dark stain will focus attention on the floor.

Here are a few of the most popular options for wood floors:

- *Natural:* Practical and easy to maintain, a natural "stain" needs only sanding, sealing, and two coats of polyurethane and will show off the actual color of the wood, darkened slightly by the polyurethane. This is a good choice for family rooms or other rooms that get lots of traffic because scratches are inconspicuous and it's simple to repair. A natural stain is also the least expensive wood finish and is appropriate for any style home.

- *Brown:* Darker wood stains are available in many shades from light brown to dark ebony. Ebony, along with Jacobean (a slightly lighter shade), are among the most popular stains for early twenty-first-century interiors. Combined with stark white walls and mahogany furniture, these stains make a dramatic statement. Most brown stains, however, are twice as expensive as natural stains, and they show scratches or damage much more easily.

- *Pickled:* To achieve the pickled look, a floor must first be sanded and bleached. A white stain is then applied—lightly or liberally, depending on how much wood grain you want to show through—followed by three coats of polyurethane. Because of the work this entails, pickled floors are about three times more expensive than those that are left natural. But, if your room is small or dark, a pickled floor will make it appear larger and lighter.

- *Paint:* Any wood floor can be painted. If yours is already polyurethaned, all you have to do is clean it, apply two coats of high-gloss oil-based floor enamel, and you're done. Most paint manufacturers now add polyurethane to their floor enamel, so there's no need to polyurethane after painting.

Gray is among the most popular colors for floors, but the possibilities are almost endless. Benjamin Moore makes fifteen ready-mixed colors and eighty custom colors; Pratt and Lambert makes only custom colors, which are generally 40 to 50 percent more expensive than ready-mixed colors. Lighter colors are almost always less expensive than darker ones. (See Resources.)

Painted floors are especially appropriate for country-style or Victorian homes. A white-painted floor with deep-colored walls makes a beautiful backdrop for white wicker furniture.

Caring for Wood

Here are a few tips for keeping your hardwood floors looking their best:

1. Sweep or vacuum regularly to remove dust and grit. Don't use household dust treatment products or furniture polish, either of which might dull the finish or make the floor slick. Instead, use a slightly damp (never wet) mop or a cleaner made specifically for wood floors.

2. Put protective felt pads on the feet of your furniture so that you can move it without denting or scratching the floor.

3. Use area rugs in high-traffic areas, especially near doorways, and avoid those with rubber backing that will prevent your

floor from "breathing." Move the rugs from time to time so that the entire floor is exposed to the light and will not oxidize unevenly.

4. Use trivets under your indoor trees or other potted plants so that the air can circulate under them. Be sure your pots and/or saucers are waterproof so that condensation doesn't damage the floor.

What, Not Wood?

There are many attractive and practical alternatives, in a wide range of prices, to wood flooring. Here are a few of the most popular for you to consider:

- *Ceramic Tile:* Durable and elegant, ceramic tile offers many possibilities. Available in one-, two-, four-, and twelve-inch squares as well as other shapes and a myriad of styles and colors, tiles are appropriate not only for kitchens and bathrooms but also for entrance foyers, dining rooms, family rooms, and even casual living rooms. If you live in a climate that's warm all year round, you might want to consider tile floors throughout the entire house. Ceramic tile is more durable than vinyl tile and needs only damp mopping to maintain it.

   The glossier the finish, the easier the tile will be on your feet. And, in heavily trafficked areas or if there are children in the family, dark grouting will be easier to keep clean.

   Ceramic tiles, properly laid, will add value to your home, so you should be sure to have the job professionally done. Not only will your floors look better; they will also last longer.

- *Vinyl Tile:* Vinyl tiles are a good choice if you don't own your home and want to update the floor of your kitchen or entrance foyer without spending too much money.

   They're easy to install and maintain, and they come in an endless variety of styles and colors. Vinyl tiles don't require waxing, and if one tile or one area is damaged, it can be replaced without redoing the entire floor. They're not as slippery as either sheet vinyl or linoleum and might be a better choice than ceramic if there are children in the house, because glasses and china are less likely to shatter when dropped by little hands.

- *Laminate:* Laminate floors are low-maintenance and a terrific choice if you have a young family. Warmer and softer than tile, laminate comes in a variety of styles and patterns, many of which look like real wood. (The Pergo brand is one of the most popular. See Resources.) It's also pretty easy to install yourself.

    Laminate is extremely durable but should be cleaned with products designed specifically for it. Avoid using too much water or other cleaners, never use wax or polish, and stay away from abrasive scouring products. To prevent scratches, use felt pads on the feet of your furniture and be sure to sweep, vacuum, and dust regularly.

- *Sisal:* Because of its stylish texture, classic patterns, and neutral colors, this is one of the most popular floor coverings used by decorators in their homes, offices, and show houses. It comes in light and dark natural shades as well as some colors, but sisal (or coir) is extremely fragile (even water will stain it) and it cannot be cleaned. Installed wall-to-wall or bound as a rug, it is best used where there is not heavy traffic, pets, or children. It is in the same price range as carpeting.

    Note: Bamboo stalks are now being used as a natural floor covering. Laid wall-to-wall or as a rug, these plaited strips are more durable than sisal, but also best suited to homes where there are only adults.

- *Marble and Granite:* These are beautiful and elegant but expensive choices. If you own your home and have the budget, you should certainly consider them. Either one would be wonderful for an entrance foyer, a kitchen, a bathroom, or a dining room, and they're both available in a wide range of colors.

    Marble is more porous than granite and, therefore, stains more easily. Both marble and granite must be sealed after installation and resealed every twelve to eighteen months, depending upon the amount of foot traffic in the room. If your marble floor becomes dull after five or more years, it can be polished to revive its natural shine.

    To maintain either marble or granite, dust regularly and wash the floor with cool, clean water or marble cleaner.

- *Slate:* Although it's not as popular as either marble or granite, slate is another durable, low-maintenance option that's suitable for entrance foyers. A sealer, wax, or an impregnator can be applied to give it a smoother finish if you wish, and it's easy to keep clean simply by mopping.

- *Cement:* This is the most cutting edge of all the flooring options, and if you have a modern home, its sleek minimalism and easy care might just appeal to you.

Poured concrete can be mixed with color added, can be shaped into patterns, and even studded with stones. It's durable and water-resistant, but, like all hard floors, it can be fatal to fallen glass or china. And, once installed, it is difficult and expensive to remove.

Preventive Care

Just as you protect your teeth with regular cleanings, you can avoid the trouble and expense of having to sand your wood floors every few years. Here's the secret—every other year, apply two or three coats of a good-quality satin polyurethane like Street Shoe (unless you prefer the high-gloss "bowling alley" look). By doing this, you'll avoid wear and tear on the wood as well as the dusty cleanup that's required after sanding.

And by the way, always sand your wood floors *after* painting the walls to avoid heartbreaking—and costly—splatters

Nonslip Wood

Waxed wooden floors can be slippery. If you're leaving your hardwood floors exposed, just keep them sealed with satin polyurethane after they have been sanded and stained. This less slippery finish will protect both the floors and those who walk on them.

Covering Your Tracks

Is a small area of your wooden floor irreparably stained or damaged because it's in a high-traffic area, such as just inside the front door? If you don't have the budget (or the inclination) to replace the entire floor, here are three less expensive alternatives:

1. Have an artist paint a decorative rug or runner over the damaged area to camouflage it. Finish with a coat of polyurethane.

2. Paint the entire floor with deck or floor paint. This is something you could even do yourself.

3. Install durable, flat-weave, wall-to-wall carpeting that will withstand heavy traffic.

How to Avoid Carpet Crumbs

If you eat every meal in your dining room, choose an easy-care wood or laminate rather than a rug that can be a crumb catcher. For an interesting effect, paint a border on your wooden floor around the area where the table and chairs are set, and protect the design with a coat of polyurethane.

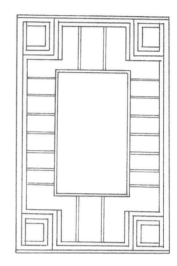

Fiber Basics

Here are the basic types of carpet fibers:

1. Wool—Soft and very resilient, wool is also expensive. It is available in many colors and cleans well.

2. Nylon—Wear-resistant; nylon withstands heavy traffic and conceals stains and soil well.

3. Blends—Wool and nylon are the best combination for durability and softness.

4. Polyester—Soft, but not as durable as nylon.

5. Olefin—Colorfast, but soils easily.

6. Acrylic—Good for areas where there are moisture problems, such as the bathroom, this carpeting is not as attractive as nylon.

Carpet Chorus

There are several types of carpeting available today. Before making a purchase, consider the needs of your family and the style of your home.

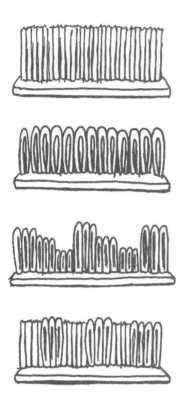

1. *Cut pile:* Loops that are cut, leaving each yarn tuft exposed on top. Not as durable as others. Includes *plush,* which has a smooth, level surface and is appropriate for traditional or formal homes, and *Saxony,* which is very popular and slightly less formal, with twisted yarn ends that minimize footprints.

2. *Uncut, level loop pile:* This carpet is durable and, therefore, excellent for high-traffic areas. It creates an informal look and includes the Berber-style carpeting. Many of the tighter commercial-style carpets that are used for residences are in this category.

3. *Multi-loop pile:* Two or three different loop heights create a dimensional look that is casual and durable.

4. *Cut and loop pile:* A variety of textures create a sculptural look. This carpet is good for high-traffic areas.

Accurate Measuring

To figure out how many yards of wall-to-wall carpeting you need, multiply the length times the width of the room and divide by nine. Add 10 percent and you'll have a fairly accurate total.

Commercial Carpeting Makes the Grade

No matter what kind of floor coverings you choose for other areas, use only commercial-grade, flat-weave carpeting on staircases. Whether you opt for a runner or stair pads, this durable carpeting will last twice as long as other types. Commercial carpeting is also ideal for high-traffic hallways and vestibules. If you prefer a rug or runner, you can always have a piece of carpet cut to the size you would like and bound. (Most hallway runners are three and a half feet wide.)

Too Many Cover-Ups

Use rugs on wood or tile floors only. Do not lay a rug on top of wall-to-wall carpeting. It's not only uncomfortable and unsafe to walk on, but it also looks as if the rug is concealing a worn or stained area on the carpet.

Stopping the Persian Wars

Use only one rug per room to define the central area, and leave the rest of the floor exposed. Two or more rugs tend to chop up the space, and most times they clash not only with one another but also with the other patterns in the room.

If two or more rooms—such as the living room, dining room, and foyer—open directly onto one another, do not use a rug in every area. Consider leaving the floor in the dining area bare and putting just one rug in the living room. This will better define the individual spaces and will make each one more distinctive. In the foyer, a simple rug that coordinates with the colors in the living-room rug or a bare floor would be best.

Spring Cleaning

If you have area rugs scattered around the house, consider removing them when the warm weather arrives. It's the perfect opportunity to have your rugs cleaned, and they can then be stored until autumn comes. The exposed wood floors will give your home a cooler look, and they'll feel great on your bare feet.

Don't Get Cold Feet

If you have a large area rug that's going to waste, use it in a bedroom with a wood floor. In many cases it will take up enough of the floor space to almost look like wall-to-wall carpeting while making the floor warmer and the whole room cozier. An 8' x 10' rug placed crosswise under a queen-size bed will extend far enough beyond both sides of the bed to give each person a bit of warm rug to step onto in the morning.

A "Square Rug" in a Round Room

Most rooms are more or less rectangular, and one that isn't can present a difficult decorating challenge. That was exactly the problem for one of my clients, whose living room had two straight walls perpendicular to one another, and a curved third wall that met the two straight ends so that the room was the shape of a quarter circle.

The longer straight wall was twenty-two feet in length, and the curved wall had five large windows running from one end to the other, with a small air-conditioning unit jutting out in the center. The entrance was in the corner where the two straight walls met. No matter what she tried, my client couldn't seem to find a comfortable configuration for her seating.

Her sofa had a curved back that extended out more than a foot at the top. Because it couldn't be placed flat against a wall without taking up too much space, she had positioned it at an angle in the center of the room with a coffee table in front of it. Underneath

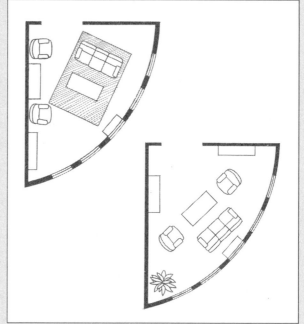

the sofa was an eight-by-ten-foot needlepoint rug whose straight lines only served to highlight the curve of the third wall and make the room feel more awkward. That rug was the biggest decorating problem in the room.

As soon as we removed it, the whole space opened up. I advised my client to leave the floor bare or to cover it with a neutral, flat-weave, wall-to-wall carpet that would provide warmth underfoot without emphasizing the odd configuration of the room. Sometimes no rug is the best option of all!

Shh—We're Sleeping

Use either wall-to-wall carpeting or a runner in the hallway that leads to your bedrooms so that the sound of clicking heels won't disturb those who are sleeping.

CHAPTER 8

Art, Accessories, and Finishing Touches

What is it that makes decorating with art so difficult to get right? Perhaps it's like finding someone to love. First comes the search. We look all over for a piece to fall in love with. We want it to make us smile and feel good every time we see it. And we want to feel that we can live with it comfortably for a long time—that the "marriage" is going to be permanent. That's where we seem to run into trouble. It's too big, it's too small, it's too wide, it's too narrow—suddenly, reality sets in and we see its limitations and "faults." But, as in any loving relationship, we must be willing to compromise.

And, whether you are a tag-sale junkie with a penchant for knickknacks or a minimalist who abhors excess, there are probably things you enjoy displaying in your home. Depending upon the presentation, either a single conversation piece or a large collection of your art and accessories can have a great impact on the space where they are displayed.

Just as there are decorating secrets for hanging your artwork, there are ways to make your collections and accessories shine. For example, a large collection kept all in one place will be less obtrusive than just a few pieces scattered carelessly around the room. Attention to detail pays off. And, if you are selective and rotate your accessories seasonally, being flexible will provide both you and your home with more space.

Whenever I ask a client if there are any accessories she can do without, I'm surprised to find that she invariably removes all the cutesy bric-a-brac and leaves only the finest pieces. So why was she displaying those pieces she knew were not enhancing her home? Perhaps because we are all constantly torn between sentimental knickknacks and simply beautiful decorative accessories, many times we wind up with an eclectic mélange of decorative pieces. As long as we keep shopping and collecting, we must also continue to edit our possessions.

Avoid Visual Overload

One mistake most people make is to hang literally every piece of art they own on every available wall, including those tiny slivers around doors and windows. The Victorians were very fond of this kind of display, but today most people are looking for a more serene feeling to their rooms. If your artwork is creating visual chaos, here is a simple approach to achieving artistic serenity:

1. Remove all the art from the walls.

2. From all the art you now have, select just the pieces that will fit well onto the space you have. (See other tips in this chapter for choosing and hanging art.) This may mean dividing the art into groups. The first will be those that work together thematically, stylistically, or whatever, and that you will rehang immediately. The second group may be pieces that would be more appropriate for different seasons, as you change the look of your room, or that would be better suited to other rooms in your house. The third may be those pieces that have outlived their usefulness and can be donated, sold, or recycled.

3. Rehang the pieces from your first selection. (Keep in mind the three rules for displaying art, listed below, and see the other secrets in this chapter.)

Art in Three Acts

1. Designate one wall to be an "art-free" zone that will create a resting place for the eyes. Note that windows with a view—or not—are "living art." So, if one wall has a large picture window, that would not serve as your art-free wall. You would probably use your longest wall for hanging a large piece of art or a grouping of smaller pieces, and choose one of your smaller walls to remain art-free.

2. Avoid hanging art on a wall less that 36" wide, or on the narrow spaces around windows and doors. Do not count these narrow spaces as your art-free walls.

3. No matter at what height you want to hang your art, whether it's a single piece or a grouping, lower it by three inches. (Yes, this rule of thumb works! And it's a better guide than trying to determine "eye" level.)

Artwork Going Up

Let the architecture of your home help dictate where to hang your art. For example, if you have a winding, narrow staircase, hang a long vertical grouping on the wall going from one floor to the next. Six narrow botanicals hung in pairs, or three vertical black-and-white photos framed in black and hung one above the other will look elegant and appropriate for the space.

Group Elegance

One of the most dramatic and elegant ways to display art is by grouping together six pieces in matching frames. Use inexpensive botanical prints, illustrations from gardening magazines, or perhaps pressed and dried leaves and flowers. Small, inexpensive, natural or black wooden frames will look fine when hung in two rows of three for a horizontal arrangement or three rows of two for a vertical grouping. You might even be able to "recycle" frames from artwork you didn't re-hang after taking it all down to evaluate your collection.

Artistic Abundance

A prominent African-American politician and his attorney wife called for help with their living room and entrance foyer.

Scattered all around their home, on almost every wall, were signed photographs of the pair with prominent black leaders from the United States and around the world. In addition, there were autographed photos of many African-American celebrities and large oil paintings, all mixed together throughout the space. In short, there was simply too much.

Our first order of business was to remove all the artwork from every wall in both the living room and foyer. Once the walls were bare, we took stock of which ones would benefit most from hanging artwork and which would be better left bare.

We hung the largest painting, a fifty-four-inch-wide by thirty-six-inch-high landscape in a beautiful, wide, flat, gold-leaf frame centered above the sofa in the living room. One of the walls in this room was comprised entirely of sliding glass doors, which we counted as "living art" because the eye is drawn to the doors just as it would be to hanging artwork. The third wall, across from the sofa, held a dramatic limestone fireplace over which we hung a smaller oil of an African woman and child dressed in the brightly colored garb of their country.

The fourth side of the room was composed mostly of pocket doors, with two narrow pieces of wall on either end. We left these small spaces bare to provide a tranquil resting place for the eyes—something that every room needs.

We then moved on to the large group of photos. Most of them were in simple black wooden frames, so we decided to reframe those that weren't in black frames to create a more uniform look.

The entrance foyer was made up of a small vestibule that opened into a large, gracious gallery. One wall of the gallery held a coat closet and a corridor leading to the study and kitchen. But the left wall was one long, unbroken expanse with no architectural breaks. This wall screamed, "Put all of the photos here!"

When we finished an hour later, we stood back to admire the impressive grouping. The entire long wall was covered from top to bottom and end to end with pictures, creating the dramatic focal point the entrance had previously been lacking.

As the woman examined over our handiwork, she said, "It's funny. I had forgotten about a lot of these photos." Her husband, always the politician, replied, "Yes, I was just thinking how helpful this will be in two years when I'm up for reelection."

Shape Shifting

If you have a large wall that is screaming for a tall, vertical piece of art but everything you own seems to be horizontal, don't rush out to buy a big, expensive new piece. Try hanging three smaller, horizontal pieces of almost the same size one on top of one another. Ideally, they should be framed in the same finish, but the frames don't have to be identical. Leave two to three inches of space between each piece.

Windows: Living Art

Large sliding glass doors, a picture window or a row of large windows, or big French doors are likely to be the focal point of any room. Therefore, it is very important that one large wall be left totally bare so that the eye is not overwhelmed by having to focus on too many places. In many of the homes I've decorated, the client and I left the wall above the sofa art-free, even if the sofa was not facing the windows, so that a dramatic view would have no competition and the room would feel more tranquil.

If your room has lots of windows and doorways, you might want to hang one large painting or grouping on one wall and leave the other ones bare.

Keeping Things in Perspective

If you're hanging a mirror or a piece of art above a commode or console that is standing next to a tall piece of furniture, such as an armoire or wall unit, be sure to hang a painting that is almost as high as the commode. This will help to balance the tall unit so that it does not dwarf the smaller piece of furniture.

Windows as Art / Art as Windows

Although you should avoid hanging art right next to *any* window, this is particularly important to remember if you have a stained-glass window. The two will constantly fight for attention, and neither will receive as much as it deserves.

Lower Your Sights

When you display a piece of art on the wall behind a lamp, vase, or a piece of sculpture, don't hang the art above the object on the table! Wall art should be hung as if there were nothing in front of it, lower than you probably think. The table piece will not distract from it, as the art will be viewed from several angles.

Only the Finest Need Apply

Use only your best artwork to create a more formal look in your living room. Watercolors, oil paintings, and pen-and-ink drawings will all enhance a sophisticated room. Framed jigsaw puzzles, prints, or children's artwork are better suited to a family room, den, bedroom, or hallway.

No Food in the Bedroom, Please

Is your art hanging in the most appropriate room of your home? Drawings, paintings, and prints will affect the mood of the space they inhabit, depending upon their subject matter, so keep the visual reference consistent with the function of the room they are in.

Place food- or drink-related pieces in the dining room or kitchen, romantic or sensual paintings in the bedroom, and dramatic or lively pieces in the living room.

Not All Art Is Painted

Many of us have seen a kimono displayed on a bamboo pole, but not all of us happen to have a kimono worthy of hanging. Why not drape a shawl, or a pair of shawls, from the pole? Or hang two small poles side by side with one shawl on each. Even simple ones will create a dramatic visual effect. Just be sure the fabrics are not doing battle with other fabrics in the room.

Flying Saucers

A collection of decorative plates makes an effective wall display, so don't scatter in different locations, where the effect will be lost. You can even get "invisible" plate hangers that will make your plates appear to be floating in space. (See Resources.)

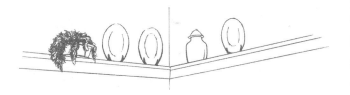

Hang plates in groups, or hang them in a line around the top of the walls of the dining room to create a unique but unobtrusive border.

A Fitting Memento

A client who had just inherited a number of paintings from her parents' estate took me into her bedroom to show me a portrait of her mother as a young woman. "Although I have many valuable and beautiful pieces from my parent's home," she said, "this painting has great sentimental value for me." Framed in magnificent gold leaf, the oil showed a lovely blond woman wearing an elegant, strapless evening gown.

"The only problem is that I feel guilty about hanging this painting in the living room because I don't have one of my father, to whom I was very close."

When I asked the client if she had anything that had belonged to him, she said, "Only his violins" and pointed to two black cases on the floor. We opened them and found two violins in good condition, each wrapped in a velvet cloth.

"Let's go into the living room and see what we can do with these," I said. We had already finished the consultation, but there was one important spot that still needed artwork: The white marble fireplace was lacking its finishing touch.

We placed the oil painting on top of the mantel, allowing it to lean on the wall behind. Then, as the woman watched, I gently removed the violins from their cases and rested them on their sides in front of the oil painting to create a unique and sentimental grouping.

When I turned around, the woman had tears in her eyes. "I feel like we've reunited my parents," she said.

Don't Overdo

When it comes to collections, don't overdo. Limit yourself to one or two per room. If you have several, spread them throughout the house and be sure they are appropriate to the room in which they are displayed. Place the most elegant or formal collections in the living or dining room. More casual groupings should remain in the family room or the bedroom.

Picture This

Almost everyone has photographs, whether of family, friends, pets, or vacation sites. Why not display them as a very personal collection. Here are a few rules for the best way to show off your photos.

- Put them all in one place in whatever room they're in—on an end table or a pair of end tables, on a credenza, or on a piano.
- Never display photos on a coffee table, where the back side would always be on view.
- All photos displayed together should be in frames of the same material—silver, brass, steel, pewter, or wood. Silver and brass are more formal and work well in traditional homes. Wood, steel, and pewter work well in modern homes. Look at the other metal finishes in the room as a guide.
- All photos in a group should be either black-and-white or color, whatever their subject matter. Keep old sepia photos grouped with black-and-white or displayed alone.
- Keep the largest photos at the back of the display and the smallest at the front, so that all of them can be seen.
- If there are very personal photos you'd like to see all the time, create a small display on your bedside table or bureau.

- Hang large photos rather than displaying them on a tabletop. The wall behind the sofa in the den or family room would be the perfect place to hang a group of family photos. Follow the same rules for framing and hanging as you would for any art.

To Create a Chic Glass-Fronted China Cabinet

If you follow these simple rules, your display cabinet will have a more organized and elegant look.

- Choose only your best pieces—no vacation souvenirs or knickknacks that will detract from the high-quality items. (Save those "collectibles" for the rec room.)
- Set out crystal, china, and silver in separate groups on your dining-room table so that you can see exactly what you have before rearranging them in the cabinet.
- Keep different materials together on separate shelves. For example, put china on the top shelf, crystal on the center shelf, silver on the bottom shelf.
- Place the largest pieces in the center of each shelf with the smaller pieces in graduating sizes on either side.
- If you have pieces with handles, such as cups, all the handles should be turned consistently toward the outside of the shelf.
- Clean and polish your pieces regularly.

3-D Art

Do you collect demitasse cups, ceramic dogs, or wooden boxes? "Hang" a collection of these or any other small objects by placing it on a gold-leaf, painted, or wooden ledge on the wall for a truly dramatic display. (See Resources.)

Eyes Up! There's a Collection on View

A narrow shelf all around the periphery of your den or dining room a foot or so below the ceiling is an ideal way to display a collection of pottery or antiques. These collections can be changed in a flash to give the room an entirely different look.

Safety in Numbers

Three or more of almost any objects that are made of the same material can be grouped together to create an interesting display.

- Place several colorful vases together on a bare shelf for a bright accent.
- Group glass decanters on a dining-room sideboard to highlight both the grouping and the furniture itself.
- Present a small collection of objects on a lacquered or metal tray on your coffee table.

Tray Display

Aside from its primary use as a server, a beautiful wooden or metal tray is also useful as a sturdy surface for glasses, books, and other objects on an ottoman/coffee table or to hold a collection of candles on a dining table.

The Multipurpose Magazine Rack

Use a spare magazine rack to hold firewood or, if it is all closed in at the bottom, fill it with potted plants and finish the top with Spanish moss.

Please the Eye with Pairs

Pairs are always important to the design of a room, but in an asymmetrical room, they are vital. Use pairs of urns, prints, or matching porcelain figurines to create a sense of balance and make the room aesthetically more pleasing.

Light Your Fire

If you're lucky enough to have a fireplace, be sure it is well equipped to live up to its full potential as the most important focal point in the room. Before you pull out the marshmallows, check to see that you have all of the following:

- a pair of andirons
- an attractive fire screen
- a set of metal tools (usually a trio)
- a beautiful rustic twig basket or hammered-metal container to hold logs
- six to ten white birch logs
- one half or a whole cord of wood
- kindling

The finish on all the metal accessories should be the same as the finish on other metal accents in the room. Generally, brass looks best in traditional rooms while steel or black metal is more appropriate for modern spaces. Unless there is an abundance of birch wood in your area, reserve the white birch logs for display purposes only. Keeping a few in the container with your more common firewood will make the display more attractive. Also, several birch logs will look elegant stacked on the andirons when the fireplace is not in use.

For safety's sake, be sure you have the flue cleaned annually, and keep all your accessories tidy and polished.

A Mirror Makes a Good Image

An ornate antique, framed mirror makes an elegant statement in an entrance foyer. For the greatest impact, it should be hung over a beautiful chest or commode. If the mirror you have is a little too small for the space, group it with two others in assorted sizes and shapes, but in complementary styles or frames. Or flank one mirror with a pair of prints in matching frames. Hang them an inch and a half apart to keep the group unified, and you'll have a dazzling new focal point for your hallway.

But what if your foyer is actually the size of a vestibule? Hang the mirror above a small (2'-3' wide x 8"-12" deep) shelf fitted with a wood or marble top. This elegant combination will provide not only an attractive first impression but also a practical resting place for gloves, purses, or a vase with fresh flowers.

The Five Rules for Arranging Books

1. Keep hardcover and paperback books on separate shelves. Usually paperbacks go on the lower shelves and the more attractive hardcovers go in the middle or near the top.

2. Arrange the books on each shelf according to size. Look to create an overall pattern so that when the shelves are viewed from afar the books are graduating either shortest to tallest, or tallest to shortest from either end toward the center.

3. Place each book so that its spine is flush with the edge of the shelf.

4. Do not combine books and accessories on the *same shelf,* except for a pair of beautiful bookends.

5. Keep the tops of the bookcases clear.

Those closet "librarians" among us, who arrange their books according to author or subject matter, should still be sure to follow rules three through five.

Deep Thinking

Most bookcases are twelve inches deep and will hold a single row of books, but what do you do with the extra space when shelves are much deeper? You have two choices: First, you could store

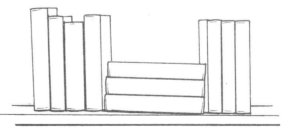

the paperbacks you have already read behind your hardcovers. The second option would be to keep small storage boxes filled with photo negatives and/or old videotapes concealed behind the books.

An Accommodating Arrangement

Stack your oversized art books horizontally. Not only will you get more books on each shelf; you'll also be able to read all the titles easily, from left to right.

No Jacket Required

Here's a fast and easy tip for storing and displaying books in a traditional or English-style home. First, separate the hardcovers from the paperbacks. Next, remove the paper jackets from all the hardcover books and place the books on your shelves grouped according to size. The plain bindings will be easier on the eye than the brightly colored book jackets, and your library will have a more sophisticated appearance. Put all the paperbacks together on the lower shelves, where they are less visible.

P.S. Save those book jackets as they will add value to your books should you decide to sell them in the future.

Combining Books and Accessories

Once you've rearranged your books according to the above suggestions, you may find that you have space left on the shelves for some accessories. Once you determine how many shelves you will need for your books and how many will be left free, figure out a pattern for your display. For example, if you have two bays of six shelves each, you might have alternating rows—one case filled with books, top to bottom, and one case of only framed photos, top to bottom.

If you have only four empty shelves, it would be best to use the top and bottom shelves for books and the middle shelves for a collection of some kind.

The main point is to establish an overall pattern that will make your display look elegant and pulled together.

And remember to follow the guidelines for displaying accessories—like together. So each shelf should hold similar items even though you may have more than one kind of collection.

Togetherness Is Key

Save space and give your room a more cohesive look by always keeping freestanding bookcases pushed together with their sides touching. Unless you have a low piece of furniture, such as a desk or TV unit, connecting them, two or more cases should always be placed side by side.

Matching Metals

The explosion of hardware options has made it possible to find knobs, pulls, and handles in every imaginable style. The finish you choose for your hardware should be compatible with the style of your home. Brass is best for traditional homes; stainless steel or brushed chrome looks sleek in modern homes. Either of the above, plus pewter or black metal, works well in homes whose décor is eclectic.

Simply adding the correct metal accents can enhance bathrooms, kitchens, and bedrooms—in fact, virtually every room in the house. One way to give rooms cohesion is to keep hardware finishes consistent throughout your home. For example, all your doorknobs should match. (See Resources.)

A Touch of Antique Romance

An antique tablecloth thrown over your duvet cover will give your bed a romantic, old-fashioned look. Use either a solid white or a colored duvet that will peek out wherever there is eyelet or lace work on the tablecloth. Add a pair of antique pillow-cases or shams, or sew a border of antique lace on a pair of solid white cases to complete the look.

Brassy Can be Beautiful

A graphic designer needed help making his living room, dining room, and entrance foyer, all of which opened into one another, appear more cohesive while still keeping each area separately defined. Once the ten common decorating mistakes were corrected, the space immediately looked and felt better, but, as we discussed the additional accessories he would need, he pointed to the front door and said, "I wish there were something I could do to make that door look better. It's visible from the living room and the dining room, and it has always annoyed me to see that unattractive lock." The door had a beautiful brass doorknob, but the copper-colored bolt lock above it—not to mention the chrome chain latch lock—detracted from the elegance of the knob.

I told him he could correct the problem immediately by replacing the chrome chain with a brass, hotel-style security lever and adding a brass lock cover that would conceal the copper lock.

By nightfall his front door was completely outfitted in brass.

When it comes to pleasing the eye and finding tranquility in your home, no detail is too small to consider.

Dust Ruffle Decor

Here is an easy way to give your bed skirt a custom-made look. Start with a solid-colored or white dust ruffle that matches your bedroom walls. Sew Velcro tape on the back of a length of one- or two-inch-wide grosgrain ribbon that is long enough to encircle all three sides of the dust ruffle.

Next, sew Velcro tape on the dust ruffle itself, two or three inches above the bottom hem. When you have finished, simply attach the ribbon all the way around.

If you like, you can do this with two or three different ribbons that can be switched with your change of linens or mood.

CHAPTER 9

Simple Solutions
for Kitchens and Baths

I t's important to balance aesthetics and function when designing any room, but the scales tip in favor of functionality when it comes to decorating kitchens and bathrooms.

Whether we are attending to our bodies in the bathroom or our stomachs in the kitchen, we need convenience, practicality, and good organization. Of course, we want the rooms to look good, too, but "pretty" is not enough. We want time spent in the kitchen to be as enjoyable as possible, and that means having a place for everything we need and spending as little time as possible on maintenance. Sturdy surfaces and handy appliances or gadgets will help, but so does planning.

The bathroom, small as it is, gets a lot of use every day. The challenge is to make this tiny space feel like a spa, so that we emerge feeling good and refreshed.

Practicality Rules

From cabinets and countertops to appliances, long life and easy maintenance is key in any kitchen. If you're starting from scratch, you'll want to make choices you can live with over time. And, if resale is an issue, keep in mind the next owner. While you can never satisfy the tastes of everyone, save stylistic quirkiness for accessories or easily changed surface decoration such as paint or paper.

The Rule of Three

Never use more than three colors in your kitchen—and that includes steel or chrome, which "reads" as a color. You can't go wrong with white, chrome, and black. White walls, cabinets, and countertops; black and white floors; and black or chrome appliances will be easy to keep sparkling and will always look elegant.

The Well-Papered Kitchen

Particularly if your kitchen is all white, you can certainly add interest and color with wallpaper. Just be sure it's vinyl for easy care, and that there is some white in the design to coordinate with the rest of the room.

Easy-Wipe Window

If privacy is not an issue, why not leave the kitchen window "naked"? Not only will you be able to enjoy the view; you'll also be able to keep it sparkling more easily. If you do need a window covering, choose a wooden blind or a pleated shade such as the Hunter Douglas Everwood blinds that are moisture proof or the low-maintenance Duette shade. Fabric curtains will only attract grease and grime and will require frequent laundering.

Easy on Your Feet

Whether you choose vinyl or ceramic tiles—depending on your budget and how long you plan to stay in your home—be sure they're smooth and not pitted or pillowed.

Your feet will slide more easily on the surface, and you'll keep that pep in your step much longer.

Step Savers

If you're designing a new kitchen, always think in a triangle. If your stove, sink, and refrigerator form a triangle, you'll be turning in a small circle rather than running yourself ragged while you cook.

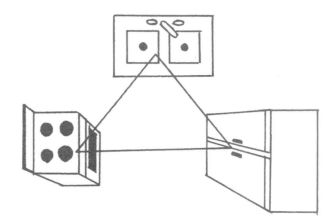

Everything in the Kitchen Sink

The ideal sink will have the following features:

- A stainless-steel bowl for easy cleaning
- A gooseneck faucet that allows you to fill or wash a large pot without having to wrestle it into the sink
- A "sprayer" for rinsing not only your pots and pans but also the sink itself
- A built-in soap dispenser that allows you to banish the bottle of dishwashing liquid from sight. If you already have a stainless-steel sink, you might have a flat "buttonlike" object on the right rear rim. That's actually a spot for the soap dispenser, which can be easily installed in about thirty minutes.

When Beauty Is Only Skin Deep

If your kitchen cabinets are out-of-date or battered-looking, you don't have to rip them all out. If the interior shelving is still in good condition, save yourself the expense of replacing by "refacing" them.

- Sometimes all you need is a coat of semigloss paint to do the trick. What was dull and grimy will become instantly shiny and bright. You can even paint Formica, so long as it is clean and primed before you paint.
- Changing the hardware can give your cabinets a whole new look. It comes in an almost endless variety of materials and styles. Just be sure you take one of the old handles along when you go to the store to be sure of the size and to confirm that the new handles can be screwed into the same holes.
- For an even bigger change, simply replace the cabinet doors with new ones from a home-furnishing or lumber store. (See Resources.)

Closed Storage

Your kitchen cabinets are closed storage, so if you do opt for glass-fronted cabinets, be sure that the glass is either sandblasted or frosted. The exception to this rule would be if you had a collection of china or glassware you wanted to show off.

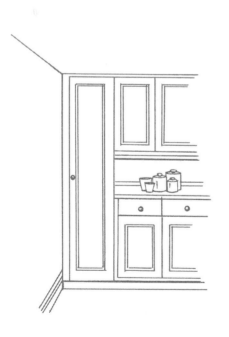

Location, Location, Location

Save time and steps by organizing the contents of your kitchen so that everything is where you need it:

- Use the cabinets closest to your sink and dishwasher to store glassware, silverware, and dishes.
- Keep spices near your stove in a wall rack or on a Lazy Susan or "steps shelves" inside the cupboard.
- Put your cooking utensils in a crock on the counter next to your stove if you don't have wall space to hang them.
- Place canned goods and staples together in one cabinet or in a pantry near the stove.

- Create a broom closet from a sliver of space—perhaps between the end of a row of cabinets and a wall. A carpenter can make a "door" that matches the finish on the cabinets and attach it to the end of the cabinets with two 180-degree hinges. Now, instead of dead space, you have a place to store mops, brooms, or even your "collection" of paper shopping bags.
- Kitchen counter space is always at a premium. Make the most of yours by getting certain items *off* the counter: Mount your paper towel dispenser above your sink; use an under-the-cabinet can opener, toaster oven, even coffeemaker; remove all decorative items, leaving only functional equipment to maximize space.

Use What You Have® of Cabinet Space

Utilize all the space inside your kitchen cabinets by using chrome cabinet organizers. These metal mini-shelves will allow you to store cups on top of plates and one row of glasses on top of another so that there is no wasted space in your cupboards.

Filling the Gap

If your kitchen cabinets do not go all the way up to the ceiling, consider filling this dead space with a row of potted ivy plants (real or silk, depending on the available light) or a group of decorative objects. Decorative boxes or tins will also provide storage space for infrequently used things. Whatever you use, make sure the accessories provide a cohesive look (such as a collection of baskets) and not just an assortment of different objects.

The Elegant Countertop

Kitchen counters not only contribute to the overall design of your space; they must also withstand a lot of wear and tear. These days, there are many choices, something to fit all tastes and every budget.

- *Formica* is the least expensive, and would probably be your choice if you're renting or planning to move on in the next few years. If you do choose this option, buy "color core" Formica. The color goes all the way through and will look better if it happens to be scraped or gouged. Formica is now better than ever before. Some varieties really look like wood, and others even simulate stainless steel.
- *Corian* is more expensive than Formica, but also longer lasting, and those nasty gouges can easily be removed with sandpaper. It is available in many colors, but choose a neutral shade, such as slate, that you'll be able to live with happily over time and that will actually add to the resale value of your home.
- *Granite* is the most expensive, but also the most elegant and durable, and if you own your home and can afford it, it might be the best option of all.

A Countertop Don't

However attractive and tempting it might be, *don't* choose tile for your countertops. The grout will discolor, you'll have trouble getting small food particles out of indentations, and you won't have a flat surface to cut on. Plus, the tiles will chip easily.

Counter Comfort

Sharp corners on kitchen and bathroom counters can be hazardous for big and small people alike. If you are installing new countertops, be sure the corners are rounded for greater safety.

Kitchen Convenience

Make your kitchen more user-friendly by following these few simple storage tips:

- Have your under-counter cabinets fitted with pullout shelves for easier access to pots and dishes.
- Place canned goods, spices, etc., on Lazy Susans so that things in the back of your cabinets and cupboards will come around when called upon.
- Install a pull-out track under the sink for your garbage pail so that the floor is left obstacle-free and the trash is not only out of sight but also easy to access.

Stash the Trash

Keep your floors clear of clutter by storing garbage pails and trash receptacles under the sink. If they must be kept out, make sure they are covered and attractive—made of metal, wood, or sleek "designer" plastic.

The Stylish Stovetop

Give your stovetop a fresh, new look by adding metal burner plates. Available in chrome, white, almond, and black, in both square and round shapes, these small covers will match the trim or color of your stove. In addition, if the burners on your stove are scratched or chipped, touch them up with heatproof porcelain touch-up paint. The paint comes in several colors and can also be used on your other appliances.

Making the Most of Your Space

If there's room in your kitchen for a small table, consider getting a round, wooden, drop-leaf model that can be placed against the wall for day-to-day use. And if you have a dinner party, you can always use it opened up in the living room or entrance foyer. A thirty-six- to forty-two-inch diameter table will fold to only twenty-four inches deep.

When the Kitchen Is Also a Playroom

A young mother hired me to help with her small apartment kitchen. The room, eleven feet long and nine feet wide, with a window on one of the short walls, did not have enough room for a standard-size table and chairs, but the woman needed some additional storage space.

She told me that space had not been a problem until they'd had their first child, who was now three years old.

Their daughter's small bedroom was right next to the kitchen. And although the woman encouraged the child to play in her room, the little girl preferred playing in the kitchen so that she could be with her mother.

What was immediately evident to me was that storage space for some of the little girl's playthings was needed.

Although the wall with the window was only nine feet wide, one of the adjacent walls right next to it had five feet of wall space before it ran into the doorway of the child's bedroom. That five-foot space was perfect for a built-in banquette with closed storage space under the seat.

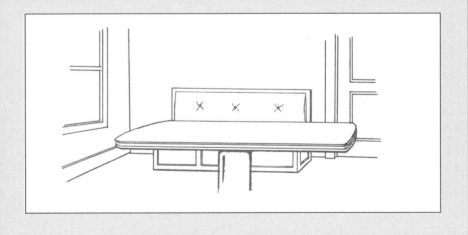

The little girl's toys could be stored inside. And with the addition of a thirty-six-inch-long by twenty-two-inch-wide rectangular pedestal table, the kitchen could also be used for eating breakfast and lunch.

I suggested that the back of the new built-in have an easy-to-clean faux leather pad and that a matching loose rectangular "leather" cushion be made for the seat, to make it more comfortable.

"This is too good to be true!" the woman exclaimed. "Storage for my daughter's toys and a place to sit comfortably with my coffee when I'm on the phone. I never would have thought of that!"

Eat-In Kitchen

Many kitchens may not be large enough for a table but will accommodate a small portable counter. With a couple of stools tucked underneath, this makes an ideal breakfast bar. And because it's on wheels, it can easily be moved to the sink or stove to provide additional workspace, or into another room to double as a bar when you're entertaining. (See Resources.)

If One Is Light, Then Light for All

If you have a light-colored floor, it's best to use a light or white stain on the cabinets to give the room a more harmonious look.

Chrome "Plated"

If your kitchen hardware is chrome, use chrome accessories as well. The same rule applies to your bathroom. Instead of using a white rubber shower caddy for your shampoos, hang a chrome caddy if all your hardware is chrome.

Kitchen Art

If your kitchen provides wall space for displaying art, remember to keep the theme appropriate to the space. Food-related drawings, posters, or floral prints always work well.

If you have only one available wall, a large clock that is two or three feet in diameter with a black or natural wood frame makes a dramatic statement. (Avoid hanging a small clock over the door frame.)

Going to the Mat

A rubber mat on the floor by your kitchen sink is good for catching spills or splashing water. And it may save you from breaking a dish or two as well.

Maddening Magnets

Many clients balk when I suggest that they remove their collection of magnets from the fridge door, but as soon as they see how much better their kitchens look, they are won over. If I've said it once, I've said it a thousand times: "No fridge magnets!" (Okay, maybe I'm overreacting a bit. . . .)

White Is Always Right

Think of the bathroom as your private spa. Keep it light, bright, and pristine. The easiest and most elegant way to achieve this look is to keep the walls, floors, and appliances white. White towels with a contrasting monogram are elegant, but if you absolutely must have color, hang towels in whatever shade you prefer, and get a matching bath mat. Not only will you have all the color you want, but you can also change the look relatively inexpensively whenever you want.

Keep Your Bathroom Whiter Than White

To freshen up your bathroom without going through a major renovation, consider having the wall tiles and bathtub spray-painted white. In just a few hours they will look like new. A word of warning, however: Don't try to do this yourself. Check your yellow pages for professionals under the heading of "Paint Spraying."

Sinks and floor tiles, which must withstand more wear and tear, tend to scratch easily when painted and are best replaced.

Bathroom Storage Solutions

Decorators love to combine elegance and organization. Here are a few tips for achieving that all-important marriage in your own bathroom.

- Build high shelving all around the periphery of the room to hold neatly folded or rolled-up extra towels or matching baskets for storing cosmetics, medicines, or hair products.
- Make sure there's a closed vanity under your sink and that it has at least a couple of shelves for storing small items rather than just one big, open space.
- Cabinets or trolleys on wheels, sold specifically for bathrooms, are ideal, assuming you have the space for one. These cabinets are closed, made of chrome or stainless steel, and can be moved for cleaning. They'll keep a multitude of bathroom essentials close at hand and neatly out of sight. (See Resources.)
- If you hang a storage unit on the wall, be sure it is closed. Open shelving looks messy if it's stacked with medicines or toiletries, and it doesn't provide real storage if it's used only to display unnecessary knickknacks.

- Replace your existing medicine cabinet, if your wall is long enough to hold one that's larger than the one you have. Or, hang a second cabinet on another wall. Many of these look like plain mirrors when closed, and some of them even have shelves on the inside of the door as well as the interior. (See Resources.)

No Place for Knickknacks

The bathroom should always be as pristine and clutter-free as possible. It's not the place for displaying knickknacks. That's why closed storage is key. Banish those open shelves that encourage displays of tchotchkes and replace them with closed cabinets that provide useful storage whenever possible.

A Cosmetic Solution

Need more room for your makeup or toiletries? If you have floor space between your sink and toilet, a chrome or brass rolling cart with shelves might be the answer.

These square or rectangular trolleys not only increase your storage space but also make it easier to see what you have. (See Resources.)

Light Up Your Face

Whether you're shaving or putting on makeup, you'll need as much brightness as you can get. If you own your home, a recessed ceiling light would be ideal for equal illumination. Lights that run down both sides of the mirror would be my a fine choice too, but if you already have a fixture over the medicine cabinet and don't want to change it, just be sure that the bulbs are frosted to cut down on glare.

Bring Down the Curtain

Solid shower curtains visually cut off a big portion of the bathroom. If you own your home, consider replacing your shower curtain with a clear glass tub enclosure. Use either brass or chrome trim to accent your existing bathroom hardware.

Renters not willing to invest in a glass enclosure can make their bathrooms look good by using a simple, solid, light-colored or transparent curtain. White is again my color of choice—moiré for a formal home or terry cloth for a more casual look. Whatever you do, don't get a busy, patterned shower curtain that will make this small room look even smaller.

You could also keep the curtain open or tie it back, but remember to keep the tub tidy because you will be exposing all those shampoos and other not-so-neat products to full public view.

The Pampered Shower

An inexpensive way to update your shower and also add value to your bath would be to treat yourself to a new showerhead. Try one of the Rain Shower heads, which are six to ten inches wide and will make you think you're standing outside in a sudden spring rain. You'll never want to get out and dry off. (See Resources.)

Too Many Towels

One solution to the problem of limited bathroom space is to hang a hotel-style wall shelf with a bar on the bottom. Fresh towels can be folded and stacked on the shelf while those in use can be hung from the bar.

Safe Harbor for Your Hair Dryer

Leaving your hair dryer on the bathroom countertop not only looks messy but can also be a safety hazard. If you can't find a drawer or cupboard to keep it in, get a wall-mounted holder for the dryer that will keep your bathroom counter uncluttered and the electrical cord away from the sink.

Rob Peter to Pay Paul

After consulting with one of the designers from my firm about redoing her master bedroom, a client took the decorator into her master bathroom and said, "Now here is a challenge for you! How can I get some storage in this tiny space?"

The designer stood shoulder to shoulder with the client in a tiny four-foot-square room with a small sink and a toilet on one side and a stall shower running the length of the other side. The sink and the toilet had recently been replaced, but the shower doors were original to the 1950s house and in poor condition. There was no room for additional storage on the wall above the toilet and sink, but the designer asked if the client would be willing to give up a few inches of the stall shower to gain some storage.

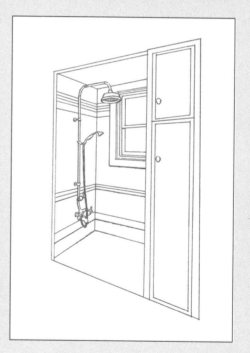

She suggested replacing the large, old double doors on the shower with a standard thirty-two-inch single door and installing a stock fourteen-inch floor-to-ceiling base cabinet in the remaining wall space outside the shower. The "new" wall between the cabinet and the remaining shower would be tiled to match the rest of the shower stall.

Handy Door Hooks

Instead of using a single, plastic hook on the back of your bathroom door, try installing a double metal hook that can be used for two bathrobes or one robe and one towel. Chrome or brass hooks that match the other metal accents in your bathroom not only look more elegant but they are sturdier, too.

Counter Productive

There's nothing more frustrating than a bathroom sink that has limited or no counter space around it. You can solve the problem by installing a narrow shelf above the sink and below the medicine chest as an alternative to those toothbrush/cup/soap holders. Just make sure it is positioned high enough above the sink so you don't knock into it every time you turn on the faucet. (See Resources.)

Be a Good Host

If you have a separate guest bathroom, you're one of the lucky ones. Please keep it supplied with guest towels of either linen or paper and a large bar of hand-milled soap. Be careful not to clutter it up with so many "decorative" objects that your guests won't have any place to put down a purse or cosmetics.

CHAPTER 10

Home Offices

Designing a work space, whether or not it is in your home, involves many of the same considerations that go into decorating a residence: placing the furniture; choosing pieces that promote comfort; creating a good traffic pattern; using artwork and accessories to enhance rather than detract from your productivity. When I started Use What You Have® Interiors in 1981, I set up an office in my home. Because I had a desk in my bedroom, that automatically became my business headquarters. Big mistake! I was never again able to relax completely in my bedroom because my "office" was never out of sight. From my bed I could see the answering machine blinking with incoming calls. Paperwork lured me into working too much on the weekend. I could never simply close the door and make it go away.

I was thrilled to see my company growing, but it took me awhile to realize that a bedroom office was not good for my health. As soon as I moved "operations" into another room, my productivity skyrocketed. And I was finally able to get a good night's sleep!

Room to Spare

If you don't have a spare room to use as an office and don't want to invade your bedroom, one solution is to place your desk *behind* your sofa. If you have the room, move the sofa off the wall and turn it to face the center of the room. Allow enough space behind it for the desk and a chair and room to move in and out. There are two benefits to this configuration:

1. The sofa will help camouflage the work area.
2. You'll automatically be facing the focal point of the room, with the best view of the fireplace, TV, or window, which will be give you a more pleasant outlook than facing a wall.

Closet Worker

If you can afford to give up the storage space, a large closet is actually an ideal place to install a home office. Everything will be neatly organized and in one spot, and you'll be able to "close the door" on your work life at the end of the day.

Pulling the Curtain on Your Workday

Living rooms, dining rooms, and spare bedrooms are good places to set up home offices. If there is enough space in one of these rooms for a desk and some files, you can create an office simply by hanging a curtain rod at ceiling height and a heavy solid curtain from one wall to another. If the room has windows on only one wall, use the side of the room without widows so you won't be blocking out light when you "close up shop." (This is also a very simple solution if the only space you have to use is in your own bedroom. Pull the curtain and your "office" is out of sight and out of mind.)

Eating at Your Desk

Dining rooms are often the most underutilized rooms in the house. In the "use what you have®" spirit, you can put this room to work as your office. In many cases there will be space in the credenza or breakfront to provide handy closed storage for your supplies.

A Successful Screen Test

A freelance Web designer needed help figuring out how to set up his home-based business. As we walked through his new one-bedroom apartment, we toyed with the idea of using his living room / dining area. The trouble was that he had so much equipment and wiring, there was no room to put it all in and still be able to use the room comfortably for living and dining.

There was, however, a closet with sliding doors in the dining area. The interior was quite deep, and there were two electrical outlets right next to it. I suggested removing the doors, setting up all his equipment inside the closet, and installing shoji screens across the entire wall. The shojis would allow him to conceal his office when he wasn't working, and they would blend nicely with the rest of his furnishings.

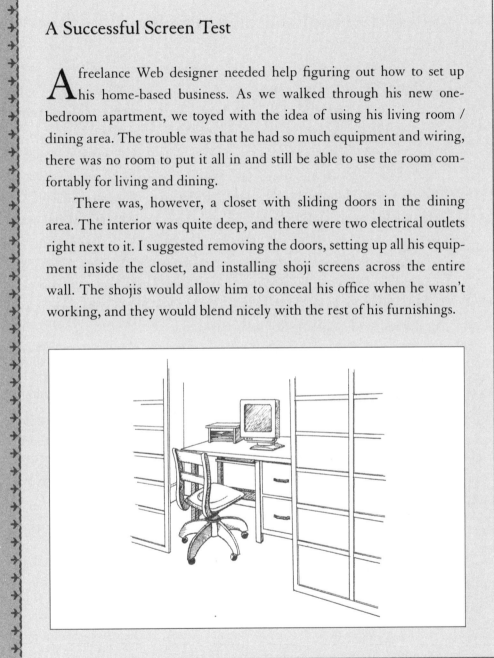

When a Problem Is Not Such a Problem

A couple who had a home-based marketing business called me in to help them make the most of their work space. When I arrived, I found that they were working at a large, oak, rectangular dining-room table, which was pushed against the wall of their dining area.

The only other furniture in that space was a small, square oak table pushed into a corner and four metal chairs. A white metal torchère lamp stood in the middle of the room, and to the right of the dining table/desk was a large double window that provided a beautiful view of the city skyline.

As we discussed how they were using the space, I learned that every night, in order to use the table for dining, they had to move the printer and fax machine as well as their laptop computer. It was not a very practical arrangement, but the solution was simple.

We turned the table around so that it stood in front of the window instead of facing the wall, and we moved the standing lamp so that it was tucked into the corner next to the table. Then we moved the printer and fax machine to the small, square table in the opposite corner. The laptop would stay on the dining table during the day and be removed for meals—a simple task. We added matching cushions to the metal chairs to make them more comfortable, and suddenly their home office became both more spacious and more practical.

Moving Right Along

If the dining-room table that you are using for a home-office desk has legs rather than a pedestal base, you can tuck two low file cabinets on wheels underneath and roll them out to another location when you have company.

Closed Storage

You can now find fully equipped, self-contained workstations that simply close up to look like a small commode at the end of your workday. All you need is a piece of wall or a corner in which to place it. Add a file cabinet on wheels to keep alongside or store in a closet when it's not in use.

Do-It-Yourself Desk

We all know you can make a desk from two file cabinets and door, but how about using two thirty-inch-high end tables that have seen better days and laying a piece of Formica or marble across the top. You can even spray-paint the tables to match the color in your room so that your "desk" will blend into the wall.

No Room to Spare

If you have no space other than your living room in which to set up an office, you can now find office furniture of all kinds—from Queen Ann desks to sleek and modern—that will fit the rest of your décor and not scream "office." (See Resources.) Or, if you don't need too much storage area, simply use a Parsons or campaign table with drawers along the top, and get some attractive desk accessories to keep on display.

Don't Mix; Match

Metal file cabinets look best if they blend with the other finishes in the room. If the colors don't match, consider painting the file cabinets with paint made especially for metal surfaces. And, if your desk and most of the other furnishings are wood, use a wooden file cabinet or paint a metal one to complement the color of the wood in the room.

Decorating Your Desk

Treat yourself to good-looking desk accessories that will keep your supplies organized and will fit well with a "home" décor. Instead of using a mug for pencils and pens, use a beautiful small vase or glass. Keep paper clips in small porcelain or crystal bowls, and use an attractive metal wastebasket, rather than a rubber garbage can.

Cutting the Cord

All those electrical cords from computers, fax machines, printers, and phones make your home office look messy. To improve the aesthetics and keep things safe, use a plastic cord cover. (See Resources.) Another option is to wrap the wires up, tie them with garbage bag twists and then tape them to the back of the closest piece of furniture.

CHAPTER 11

The Family-Friendly Home

Decades ago, plastic slipcovers were all the rage, and most people used their living rooms only for entertaining company. Holiday dinners found the adults in the dining room using the "good" silver and china, and the kids isolated in the kitchen, using the "everyday" dishes.

Things have changed. These days, everyone wants to share as much of their limited free time as possible with their family. Working mothers want to enjoy their children when they are home, and not worry about their furnishings. People with pets want to enjoy them without worrying about shedding fur and unfortunate "accidents." And, when there are older people in the household, we want them to be safe and comfortable, too.

Fortunately, there are decorating alternatives for virtually every room that will keep the entire family safe and happy without compromising the elegance of your home.

Toddler-Safe Strategies

Many people think they have to banish the breakables to a closed cabinet when toddlers are around. Not so. Simply rearrange your collections and knickknacks so that glass and porcelain collectibles are beyond reach—atop the piano or on a higher shelf, while wooden boxes, baskets, silver, and metal objects take their place on coffee tables and other child-height surfaces.

In baby's room, place soft toys and books on the bottom shelves of an open unit where he or she can reach them, and put framed photos and breakable keepsakes on the top shelves.

To Accommodate the Wonder Years

Here are a few ways to transform baby's room into a more grown-up-looking space for a small child:

1. Replace the rocking chair with a comfortable upholstered chair for reading.

2. Many changing tables are set atop a complete bureau. By removing the changing-table top and hanging wall shelves, you'll have a unit that won't need replacing for several years.

3. Replace baby prints and designs with more mature fabrics, such as plaids or stripes in the same color scheme, so that they will complement the walls and floor coverings.

4. Replace large infant floor toys with a pint-size wooden or Formica table and two matching chairs to be used for drawing and playing games with friends. Kids need a place of their own—not the kitchen counter—to play and entertain friends

5. Remove the baby wallpaper and replace it with a simple, light-colored, washable vinyl wallpaper that coordinates with the new fabrics.

Hidden in Plain Sight

Kids always seem to get the smallest bedroom in the house, and, therefore, they never have enough storage space. To store out-of-season clothing and keep toys out of sight, consider a high wooden platform bed with two to three feet of open space beneath the mattress section where you can keep closed storage bins or boxes that your child will be able to access easily.

Closed Storage for Kids

Although children do need open shelving for toys and games, they also need someplace to keep things out of sight, and the traditional toy chest or trunk may not be the best choice. Things that open upward, and can, therefore, also slam down, can be dangerous for little people. Better choices would be cabinets with sliding doors or doors that open out.

Closets That Grow

Small children need to reach their clothes so that they can learn to dress themselves, but investing in a closet your child will soon outgrow is neither practical nor necessary. Instead, you can fit the existing closet in your child's room with plastic brackets to hold a low pole for hanging clothes that can easily be moved up later on. You can also buy ready-made cubbies to hold folding clothes such as sweaters, T-shirts, jeans, sweatpants, and overalls—the clothes most young children wear every day. (See Resources.)

Sleepover Space Saver

Children's rooms need lots of play space, so instead of buying a second twin bed to use for "sleepover dates," why not get a trundle bed that will "hide" under your child's single twin? Alternatively, use an inflatable bed that can be stored in a closet when it's not in use.

Sibling Sanity

If your children are sharing a room, here are a few tips to give them a good-looking bedroom—and cut down on sibling rivalry:

- Make sure there is matching bedding—sheets, blankets, and duvet covers—on each bed.
- Center matching bulletin boards on the wall next to each bed so your kids can display their favorite photos and other pinups.
- Give them labeled storage bins in different but complementary colors to house their individual keepsakes and toys.

Color Me Soothing

Would you be able to relax in your bedroom if it were painted bright red, blue, or yellow?

Although these primary colors are fun, children need tranquility too. Consider using colors like banana, celery, periwinkle, and peach, which are still striking but also soothing. And, with the exception of peach, any of these colors would work as well for a boy as a girl.

Keep It Simple

The most practical and classic furniture finishes for any child's room are either all-white or wooden surfaces with simple lines. A bed, bureau/chest, and desk in these neutrals are suitable for either a girl or a boy and will allow you to change the colors and accessories in the room as time goes by and your child grows.

Easy-Wipe Wallpaper

The wallpaper in kitchens, bathrooms, children's rooms, and high-traffic hallways should be vinyl coated so that it can be kept clean with a sponge and mild cleanser. The vinyl coating isn't necessary in dining rooms, bedrooms, and large open foyers where stains and sticky fingers are less likely to be a problem.

Bulletin! Bulletin!

If the natural cork- and pine-framed bulletin board in your child's room doesn't work well with the rest of the decor, simply paint the *entire* surface in the semigloss color of your choice and use color-coordinated or clear plastic pushpins to display artwork and schoolwork.

Display Storage

Instead of using a wallpaper border to spiff up your child's room, have a six-to-eight-inch wooden shelf mounted twelve inches below the ceiling all around the periphery of the room. Stained or painted to match the trim or furnishings, it will provide room to display toys and stuffed animals. As with any display of "collectibles," put all the stuffed animals in one area on the shelving, all the dolls together, etc., to create an organized and attractive display that can be changed as your child grows. Remember that these shelves will be beyond the reach of a small child and should not be used for toys or games that are used on a regular basis.

Safe Seating

If you're thinking about purchasing stools for the counter in your kitchen or family room, be sure they have backs. Small children need sturdy, safe seating to help prevent falls. (See Resources.)

Safety First

The bathroom can be a dangerous place for both children and older people. Here are a few tips for making this important room both safe and comfortable:

- Place nonskid strips in the tub and shower.
- Use bath mats with a rubberized backing.
- Install countertops with rounded, not squared, corners.

Home Sweet Playpen

A couple in their late thirties called my firm two years after having their second child. Their home wasn't large but was comfortable for the four of them. They just thought it needed freshening up since they hadn't done anything to it recently, but they were daunted by the prospect of decorating from scratch.

When I arrived, their home looked like a branch of the local toy store. Both the living-room and dining-room floors were covered with toys, and there was barely a path clear enough to walk through.

The pair was clearly embarrassed about the mess and apologized profusely. They explained that they had waited several years before having their first child, and now that they were parents, they were having difficulty establishing boundaries for their children. Their older child, a girl of four, had a large bedroom of her own, and their two-year-old son had a somewhat smaller room. But somehow, the toys and baby paraphernalia kept piling up and spilling over into the "public" rooms, and the couple felt guilty about getting rid of any of it. Things seemed to stay where they dropped, and at night, after the kids went to sleep, the couple was left to relax in the living room, sharing the sofa and coffee table with their children's dolls and games. The chaos was getting to both of them.

Fortunately, they had good, durable furniture, so we began by correcting the common decorating mistakes in the living room. First we created a comfortable U-shaped conversation area with their sofa and a pair of chairs. Then we removed all the extraneous furnishings and accessories, and after selecting their favorite pieces of artwork, we rehung a couple of paintings, leaving one wall free of art to make the space feel more restful. Immediately, the room started to look and feel good, and my clients began to smile. At that point, it was time to get to the heart of the problem: How would they deal with the avalanche of toys?

First, we brought in a trunk from the parents' bedroom to replace their coffee table and double as storage space. In addition, we decided that an entertainment center would not only provide valuable closed storage, but would also neatly house the television and audio equipment that was presently on an open cart with all of its wiring exposed—posing a potential danger to children. We found still more storage in both children's bedrooms, as well as under a living-room window seat, where games could be kept in rattan baskets. And we talked about donating any toys the children hadn't used for a while to a charity for homeless children.

Last, I suggested that they institute "basket time" for the kids before they went to bed each night. The object of this game would be for the children to find all their toys and place them in a big basket within a certain period of time. If they succeeded, the children would get a reward, such as stickers or candy, plus a sense of accomplishment from tidying up the house and learning to respect their family's living space. The parents would benefit both by having fun with this "Beat the Clock" game and by reclaiming a toy-free and tranquil living room.

By the time I left that day, my clients were filling cardboard boxes with toy donations and looking forward to teaching their children the new game.

Hide the Hardware

If you have a built-in cabinet or storage closet in a high-traffic area of your home, get it fitted with touch-latch magnetic hardware. There will be no handle or knob to protrude and possibly harm a passerby, and your smooth-fronted cabinet will be virtually invisible.

No More Wide-Open Spaces

The upstairs entrance areas of many split-level homes have an open railing that can be dangerous for babies and young children.

You can protect your little ones by placing a closed credenza or commode in front of the open slats. One caveat: Be sure the back of the piece is finished with wood or a wood veneer that will look attractive when viewed from below.

Slip-Free Carefree Flooring

Both children and older people need flooring that is safe, and busy mothers need flooring that is easy to care for. Wood floors that are waxed can also be slippery; try two or three coats of satin polyurethane instead. It's less slippery than wax and will also preserve your floor. Pergo wood floor laminates are a wonderful alternative because they look just like wood and can be easily wiped or mopped when necessary. Commercial, flat-weave carpeting is a good choice for bedrooms, family rooms, and hallways where acoustics are an issue.

Preventive Plumbing

To prevent a potentially dangerous problem before it happens, install a Scald Safe faucet in the bathtub. Its built-in hot water sensor will automatically shut off the water when it gets too hot. An automatic restart button makes resetting a snap. (See Resources.)

The Shoji Solution

The high cost of housing has forced many people to stay where they are instead of moving to larger quarters after they have children. When this happens, the space that is most often compromised is the bedroom(s) of the youngest members of the family. Sharing the same bedroom is not a problem for children of the same sex, but when it's a girl and a boy who are approaching adolescence, each child needs to have a private space.

The usual solution is to divide a bedroom. If the master bedroom provides a lot more square footage and it is not too much of a sacrifice, parents might consider switching rooms and dividing the larger one for their kids. Instead of putting up a permanent wall, Japanese Shoji screens might be a better choice. Built wall-to-wall, shojis have several benefits:

1. Unlike solid, sheet-rocked walls, these lightweight wood-and-rice paper panels can be removed easily and reused in another room or home.

2. Shojis allow light to filter through in case there are windows on only one side of the bedroom. It is also possible to install windowlike sections of screen that open and close to allow for the circulation of air conditioning and heating.

3. Entire panels can be made to slide, exposing the whole room for a more spacious feeling when desired.

4. For durability, you can opt for sturdy fiberglass panels rather than the more delicate rice paper. And fiberglass also cleans easily.

5. Shoji screens are available in a natural wood, light wood, or black satin lacquered wood, or they can be painted to match the walls.

Reclaiming Your Space

A couple in their fifties called me in to help redecorate their son's former bedroom and turn it into a guest room.

We talked for a while and decided to keep the trundle bed their son had used. It would be re-covered in a sophisticated, camel-colored, ribbed ottoman fabric. We also decided to keep the long, wooden wall unit in which he had displayed his sports trophies and school memorabilia. Now that the unit was empty, I suggested that we move all the couple's books onto the empty unit to create a cozy, library look.

Next, we switched their son's chest of drawers with a desk from another bedroom, and suddenly the space felt like a study. All they would need to buy were new carpeting—we selected bamboo-colored, wool sisal—and a pair of big throw pillows in a wide camel-and-black awning-stripe fabric for the top of the trundle bed. (The black color tied into the cotton tape trim on the wooden blinds.)

Without actually replacing any of the furniture, they reclaimed and completely redecorated the room.

According to Size

If you have a standing coat rack in your front hall, consider replacing it with wall-mounted hooks. You can hang very low ones for young children so that they can learn to hang up their own jackets, and higher ones for older kids and adults. Standing coat racks are too high for little ones, and they can also topple over and hurt a small person who might be caught underneath.

Tuck Me In!

Kids sometimes forget that a shower-curtain liner needs to be inside the tub in order to keep the bathroom floor dry. If *your* children keep forgetting, give them a reminder. Make up a small, white, business-size card that says, "Tuck me in!" Have it laminated and hang it from a metal key ring loop at the end of the curtain, where the kids pull it closed. This gentle reminder will save your floors and your back. (This tip also works well for absentminded adults!)

Sight Savers

The older one gets, the more light one needs. Good lighting is especially important for seniors. Table lamps with three-way switches that go up to at least 150 watts are best. And do make sure you are using the maximum wattage in all your lamps.

Water, Water Everywhere

Is steam or electric heat making your home feel like the Sahara in winter? Humidifiers are unattractive but you can return moisture to the air with these attractive and simple alternatives, either of which will be a lot more effective than you might think. Every member of your family will feel better for it.

- Fill a bowl or compote with smooth river rocks and add water. Submerge all the stones except for a few at the top. Display the stones as you would fruit or flowers, and be sure to check the water level daily.
- If you love the sound of splashing or trickling water, use an Asian-inspired mini-fountain. It will soothe your soul along with your sinuses.

Claw No More

Here are a few fabrics cats love to claw, and a few they might pass up. Keep these in mind when you're making upholstery or carpeting choices:

Favorites

- silk, especially raw silk
- leather
- chenille
- textured fabrics
- thick, loopy rugs and carpeting

Passes

- chintz
- smooth cotton
- Ultrasuede
- velvet
- flat, tightly woven rugs or carpeting

Cat-Scratch Containment

Does your cat think the upholstered arm of your sofa or chair is his personal scratching post? If so, try placing the arm covers so that the fabric runs down the length of the arm, in front, where your feline friend tends to work on her manicure, rather than along the top. Have an extra set of covers made, if necessary, to use as a "good" set when company comes.

Recently, a client and I did the same thing when her cat turned the living-room ottoman into a scratching post. We had a slipcover made to go over the torn upholstery when she entertained, and her contented cat left the other fabrics in the room unscathed.

One Plus One Equals Two

When one our decorators had her second daughter, she found that the small bedroom the girls were to share was going to be a problem. Although they were planning to buy a house within the next two or three years, they needed to make do with the space they had for now.

The room, with one standard-size window on each of two walls and the doorway on a third wall, gave them few options for arranging the furniture in a way that would satisfy the needs of both children. The designer finally realized that the only direction she had to go was up.

Although the ceiling was only eight feet high, they built in a sleeping loft going from the back wall to the center of the room for the older child. The baby's crib and changing table were placed in the open, "nonloft" section of the room. The entire section directly under the loft was given over to big sister's bookcases, play table, and two chairs.

When the work was complete, the older girl told her mommy, "You are like a magician. Before I had one room, but you turned it into two!"

Pampered Paws

Keep a dark-colored towel on a hook by your front door to wipe your dog's feet when it is raining or snowing.

If your pet doesn't object too much to wearing booties, which will also protect her from the salt spread on the ground during snowstorms, they will save you both the trouble of toweling her down when you return home.

Removing Spot's Spot(s)

To remove pet stains and their odor from carpeting or fabrics, pour white vinegar on the offending spot and then blot repeatedly with a paper towel until the paper has absorbed all the vinegar and comes away dry. Be sure to test an inconspicuous spot first, to be sure the solution won't damage the fabric.

CHAPTER 12

Bringing the Outdoors In

In the 1970s, an amazing thing happened in the world of interior design: There was an explosion of indoor gardening. Plastic plants, so popular in the 1950s and '60s, were suddenly viewed as nothing more than unattractive dust collectors by a generation tired of anything "fake" and searching for "the real thing."

Floor plants, trees, hanging baskets, and terrariums began to appear in plant stores, nurseries, and even supermarkets. Plant lights, plant vitamins, and flowerpots in every conceivable material were available to anyone who yearned to bring the great outdoors in. Even those who complained of having a "black" thumb jumped at the chance to have their own herb garden right on the kitchen windowsill.

Today, scraggly spider plants and dead ficus trees have become a thing of the past. We still love having plants in our homes, but we've grown more realistic about the time and the space required to care for them. Savvy indoor gardeners now look for hardy, easy-care plants that will survive their owners' long vacations in rooms with limited natural light. To put it bluntly, we want plants without baggage.

Keeping It Serene

If you're an outdoor gardener, you probably know that your flower beds look best when planted with a coherent color scheme. The same idea applies to interior flower arrangements. For example, if your living room color scheme is navy, white, and pink, it's best to display flowers in various shades of pink and white. A vase of orange or red flowers would jar the eye and clash with the decor.

On the other hand, if your scheme were neutral or monochromatic, an assortment of vibrantly colored flowers would overwhelm everything else in the room. A better choice would be a vase of assorted all white or all pale yellow flowers. This simple arrangement will not disturb the serenity created by the room's muted tones.

Coordinate floral arrangements with existing fabrics, art, and paint colors for the most elegant effect.

Peace from a Tinkling Brook

If you haven't got a lot of natural light or a green thumb, the sound of water splashing from a fountain can be an enjoyable alternative. Asian-style fountains, complete with river stones, are small and simple to use, and they work well with any style interior. (See Resources.)

Carefree Indoor Gardening

Has every plant and tree you've ever owned withered away because you don't have sufficient natural light? Have you given up on keeping anything alive in your home? Here are two other options:

- Fill a brass, silver, or copper pot with a full, lush English Ivy plant and display it on your coffee table or entrance console. All you'll need to do is water it about once a week and enjoy it!

- For an even more carefree option, create a treelike effect with live curly willow branches! Fill a large tabletop urn, floor urn, or vase with lots of these fresh curly branches. When you purchase them, they will be soft and may have a few leaves, but it isn't necessary to add water. Your new "tree" will dry naturally, and it requires absolutely no care. Simply place it in a corner of your living room, dining room, or foyer, on a pedestal on the floor or centered on a mantel or sideboard, and enjoy it.

Orchid Afterlife

Do you love phalaenopsis orchids as much as I do?

Although they flower for two to three months when in season, there's a way you can "extend" their bloom. After the last blossom has died, cut the remaining stem back to just below the spot where the lowest flower was. Purchase a white silk orchid and some raffia string. Put the stem of the silk flower next to the stem of the live plant, so that they overlap by one inch. Wrap the two stems together with the raffia string until you can't see where one ends and the other begins. Tie the raffia in a bow and snip off the excess. Continue to water your orchid with warm water once a week while it is dormant. When new buds appear in six months, remove the silk flower. There's nothing more elegant than a simple white orchid on the coffee table.

Designer Indoor Greenery

Here's a fast and easy way to add elegance to the indoor greenery you already have. Purchase a bag of potting soil and a bag of Spanish moss at your local florist or nursery.

Add some new soil around the base of the plant and then some moss on top of the soil in each pot. The moss will give your plant a more finished and elegant look.

Display Plants Like Objects d'Art

To display small plants most effectively, use containers that are made of the same material—all terra cotta, all brass, or all ceramic—and group the plants on a decorative tray or in a basket.

Say It with Flowers—and Candles

One of the simplest, most elegant statements can be achieved by setting a pair of silver candlesticks on either side of a silver vase filled with flowers. White flowers and white candles or pale, celery-colored candles and a green Lady Slipper orchid in a silver mint-julep cup lend an air of refinement to any tabletop.

If you love candles but are concerned about dripping wax on your rugs, tablecloths, and tabletops, here's how to remove those inevitable "wicked" spills. Cover the stained area with a piece of brown paper and iron it, using the coolest setting. The wax will gradually adhere to the paper, leaving your floor or furnishings spatter-free.

Mini-Gardens All Over the House

To create an indoor mini-garden, cluster several floor plants together, or group one or two medium-size potted plants around a tall tree. Placed in the corner of a living room, dining room, or foyer and lit with accent lights, this garden makes for a very dramatic display—and it's an ideal way to fill an awkward corner space in a room or to balance other pieces of furniture.

The Longer, the Better

When you're buying cut flowers, you want them not only to look beautiful but also to last. Here are a few long-lasting varieties of cut flowers for you to consider:

1. chrysanthemums
2. orchids (dendrobium)
3. lilies
4. amaryllis
5. tuberoses
6. carnations

The Kindest Cut of All

Here are a few ways you can prolong the life of your cut flowers:

1. Always wash your vases with antibacterial soap.

2. Check the water level in your vase daily, and replenish it with lukewarm water.

3. Keep arrangements away from cigarette smoke and from fruits and vegetables that emit ethylene gas.

4. Keep flowers away from direct sunlight and warm surfaces, such as the top of your television.

Floral Life-Extension Magic

Here is a surefire way to help preserve cut flowers without those little packets of commercial mixtures to keep your blossoms fresh and beautiful for the longest time possible: Fill half the vase with lukewarm water combined with one or two drops of Clorox bleach, then fill the rest of the vase with 7UP or Sprite (don't use a generic soda, which is yellow, not clear).

A Rosy Future

Have you ever wondered why the beautiful roses you buy always seem to die without opening their buds? The culprit may be cold water and stem injury. Try this: When you bring home the roses, prepare a vase with warm water. Remove all the leaves that will be below the waterline, and cut the stems on an angle, under water in the kitchen sink or in a large tub, with a sharp knife (never regular scissors). The angled cut will ensure that each rose gets water no matter where the stem sits on the bottom of the vase. Quickly, place the cut roses in the vase. Be sure not to expose the cut flowers to the air for more than three seconds after cutting the stems or the air will create a seal that will prevent the stems from absorbing sufficient water.

Gather Ye Flower Beds

If you are cutting flowers from your garden to use inside your home, remember the following points:

- Gather flowers in the early morning or in the evening. Flowers cut in the afternoon will have a much shorter vase life.
- Carry a bucket of warm water into the garden with you. As you cut each flower, place it in the water immediately. Never put the cut flowers directly on the ground, where they can become contaminated.
- Once the flowers are inside, recut the stems on an angle in the kitchen sink under water, then allow them to sit in a bucket of warm water with a few drops of Clorox bleach for a minimum of two hours. Arrange the flowers in a vase, but do not expose the cut ends to the air for more than a few seconds.

Adding a Touch of Class

Two ideas to give your floral arrangements a professional touch:

1. Inside a plain glass vase, place a small branch of fresh, soft curly willow so that it circles the interior of the vase once or twice. Then add water and flowers, and enjoy.

2. Wrap a large green banana leaf around the outside of a vase, and tie it securely with a piece of natural raffia. This wrap will disguise even the cheapest container and create an instant decorator look. (In fact, you can wrap a vase in any decorative paper or cloth to achieve the same effect.)

A Vase by Any Other Name

You can use almost any container for flowers, as long as you have a glass that will fit inside it. Fill the glass with water and arrange your flowers in it. Set the glass in the container of your choice and add some Spanish moss, if necessary, to conceal the glass. Baskets, Asian boxes, bowls, cups—any attractive holder—will create an interesting display for your posies.

Create Your Own Container

Make your own vase by lining any kind of container with the bottom half of a clear, one-liter plastic soda bottle. To do this, simply cut off the top half of the bottle and set the bottom half inside the container of your choice. Fill the bottle with soil or water, arrange your plant or flowers, and finish off the top, if necessary, with Spanish moss to conceal the bottle or soil.

Bamboo Elegance

Bamboo sticks and natural raffia string make an attractive and effective way to stake potted plants instead of the common green wooden sticks and twist ties that are provided by the plant store.

It's All Arranged

To create an attractive mixed-flower arrangement every time, just follow these few simple steps:

- Choose a vase appropriate to the size and height of your flowers.
- Fill it with water of the appropriate temperature— cool for bulbs; warm for roses; lukewarm for all other varieties—and add a preservative.

- With a sharp knife or flower shears, remove all the leaves that will be below the waterline.
- Starting with the tallest flowers, cut each stem on an angle with a sharp knife under water.
- Place each stem in the vase with the tallest in the middle, shorter ones in a circle around them, and the shortest ones around the edge of the vase.
- Continue to add and integrate your flowers until the arrangement has a uniform shape.
- Add greens last.
- If the arrangement looks sparse, add Spanish moss along the neck of the vase, dripping down a bit to fill in the base.

Form Should Follow Function

Make sure your flower arrangements fit the place where they will be displayed. If the arrangement is to be placed in the middle of the dining-room table, not only must it be low enough for diners to "see over," but it also needs to look good from all sides. Turn the vase as you assemble the arrangement so it comes out well balanced. An elegant and easy alternative would be to "float" a few stemless flowers, such as roses in full bloom, in a glass bowl. Guests will be able to see "through" as well as "over" the centerpiece.

If the bouquet is to be placed on a shelf or against a mirror, you can make the backside flat. (If you are going to display flowers on a small table against a wall, however, place the arrangement in the middle of the table, rather than pushed to the back.)

Creating a Floral Illusion

If you have a mirrored wall or a large, framed mirror with a table or chest below it, place a flat-sided, flower-filled vase against the mirror and your arrangement will look twice as big as it actually is.

Faux Ficus Foliage

In addition to her ability to transform a home from something blah to something beautiful, the most senior designer with my firm also has a green thumb.

She has always been successful at raising beautiful plants—until, that is, she met her match—the ficus tree. Now, in her defense, everyone who bought a ficus tree in the 1980s was fighting a losing battle. The trees, which were cultivated in ideal conditions in Florida, were shipped to cities all around the country where the climates were totally different from what the trees were accustomed to. The result was that all the unknowing, innocent people who fell in love with their beautiful, shiny almond-shaped foliage and lovely white, twisted trunks were left with a floorful of leaves and a tree that had none.

But that didn't deter my colleague. She was ready when her ficus tree started to bite the dust. She was going to have the last laugh. Every time a leaf fell off her tree, she simply whipped out her trusty hot glue gun and replaced the deserter with an identical silk one. Within three months, every branch was covered with lifelike green silk ficus leaves, and no one even realized the difference. When her friends asked how she managed to keep such a temperamental tree in such good shape, she simply replied, "I just keep sticking with it."

Too Big for Its Place

As glorious as a huge bouquet can be, if it's too large for the table it's sitting on, it will look odd. If you have a lot of flowers, make two complementary arrangements that can be displayed on a shelf, on end tables, on a console, or at opposite ends of a long mantel. (You know how important pairs and proportion are to Use What You Have® decorating!)

Going Dutch

Tulips look wonderful when displayed in one bunch of the same color on your coffee table or in two bunches on your entrance commode. Try mixing them with freesia in the same color for a delightful and fragrant bouquet. To extend the life of the tulips, place three pennies in the bottom of the vase and use cool, not warm, water.

Tending Tall Tulips

Have you ever noticed that your tulips seem to go straight up several hours after you've arranged them in your vase, rather than bending over in graceful curves? Here is a tip on how to keep them from standing at attention:

As you place each tulip in the vase, pierce the stem once at the very top, right below the petals, with a straight pin. This will keep your tulips in their original arrangement.

CHAPTER 13

Change for All Seasons

Just as you prefer to wear heavy woolen clothing in the winter and cool cotton or linen in summer, so, too, does your home benefit from seasonal change.

Depending on the amount of time and energy you have, you can do this either twice or four times a year. Either way, your rooms will be more comfortable for you, and you'll have fun "shaking things up" a bit to enjoy a fresh look, especially if you live in the same place twelve months a year.

Every room in your house will be renewed, and you won't have to spend a lot of money. You'll find that these seasonal mini-makeovers offer a big payoff for a relatively small investment, and your fresh habitat will seem less of a habit and much more fun.

Cooling Down Your Décor for Hot Summer Days

When it's time to convert your home for the warmer weather, here are a few "cool" ideas:

- Transform velvet, needlepoint, and woolen throw pillows with cotton or linen slipcovers.
- Put away woolen or chenille afghans.
- Slipcover upholstered furniture in lightweight fabrics, such as cotton or linen.
- To change the look of your bedroom, use a cotton duck slipcover for your upholstered headboard to put over the heavier, darker fabric you use in the winter.
- Roll up heavy rugs and replace them with sisal or coir, or simply leave the wood floors bare.
- Put away heavy, dark accessories and display summery pieces such as baskets, seashells, and white or light-colored candles.
- Replace winter-themed artwork with lighter pastels.

Fanning the Flames

Does the warmer weather start you thinking about how lovely it would be to feel the breeze from a ceiling fan as you sip your iced tea? If the answer is yes, here are a few important points to keep in mind.

- If you're planning to use a fan for only three or four months and you have to remove the existing overhead light fixture to accommodate it, don't sacrifice your lighting. Buy an attractive floor or table fan instead, and store it away when it's not in use. You'll have good light all year long and a breeze whenever you need it.
- If you need extra cooling year-round, a ceiling fan can help, but avoid the type with built-in lights. Ceiling fans that have built-in lighting generally come with inexpensive-looking metal "cans" or globe lights that cast very unattractive shadows. There are many stylish fans without lights that will not compromise the aesthetics of your home. (See Resources.)

Tip Your Hat to Spring

Your entrance area announces both the style of your home and the season of the year every time the front door opens. Before you put out a vase of daffodils, here's a suggestion for an imagina-tive and practical way to re-fresh this important area for spring.

If your foyer or hall-way has a standing coat rack, a hat rack, or simply large hooks for hanging jackets and other outerwear, start by removing all that winter gear. Once you've cleared every-thing away, pull out your straw, cotton, and baseball hats. Hang these lightweights in place of your woolens, along with several sheer or gauzy scarves, and suddenly your en-tryway will silently let your guests know that spring has arrived in your home.

Everlasting Spring!

To preserve dried roses, spray them with hair spray. Use them to create dried flower arrangements or to adorn a straw hat.

Summer Slipcovers

Have simple cotton or linen slipcovers made for pieces that are upholstered in che-nille, velvet, wool, or nubby fabrics. Choose the lightest color in your color scheme or just use a solid off-white fabric to create a cool, comfortable, airy look for summer. At the end of the season, simply remove the slipcovers and have them cleaned and stored away to await another spring.

Some Ties Don't Bind

If you purchase ready-made slipcovers with ties on the front of the arms, have the ties removed. Most ties do not secure the covers and simply make them look sloppy. From a decorating point of view, unless you have a casual country-style house, shabby chic is really passé.

Give Your Pillows the Slip

Transform the look of your throw pillows for fall. From November through April, slipcover light chintz solids, summery floral prints, or brightly colored cottons in darker cotton or linen velvet. Or, if you prefer, you can use a nubby, textured fabric to create a cozier look. Remember to pick up your throw pillow color(s) from your rug or an existing fabric for a cohesive look.

Winter Woolies

In addition to using flannel sheets to keep you cozy in winter, put a lamb's-wool mattress cover on your bed. Not only will you feel warmer, but your bed will also be softer and more comfortable.

"Purr-fect" Luxury

Decorate your sofa with a luxurious cool-weather accessory, a faux-fur throw that will also keep you cozy in the winter. They come in various "furs" and are lined with soft velour. (See Resources.)

Accessorize for All Seasons

In the autumn, collect a large bunch of leaves in as many colors as you can find. Spread them across your dining-room buffet or entrance commode along with the accessories that are already there. Display a bunch of bittersweet branches in a large vase or urn in you living room, and place a group of tiny pumpkins or gourds around its base or near it, filling a compote.

For Christmas, exchange the leaves for pine branches and replace the gourds with pinecones.

As spring and summer roll back around, use flowering branches, seashells, or river rocks to change the look again.

Decorator, Light My Fire!

A gentleman with whom I had worked previously called me in to consult when he and his new wife bought a condominium.

His previous apartment, which was in a town house, had not just one, but two fireplaces. Now that he and his wife had moved to a modern building, he was already mourning the loss of winter evenings reading by a crackling fire—and it was only July.

Although we couldn't install a real fireplace, we decided to do the next-best thing. The couple purchased a beautiful marble mantelpiece that we centered on the longest wall of the living room. We then painted the section of wall inside the mantel black, to simulate a fireplace opening. The "look" was completed with a stack of electric logs, a pair of antique andirons, and a rustic twig basket filled with white birch logs. When everything was in place, we scattered a few of the birch logs over the electric ones and, with the click of a switch, the room was lit by the glow of the "fire." "So tell me," my client said, smiling, "do you have a source for room spray that smells like burning logs?"

Aromatherapy

A home must smell good, as well as look and feel good in all seasons. To make your home more inviting, keep something scented on your entrance chest or shelf. Fresh flowers in spring and summer, dried eucalyptus or cinnamon sticks in a bowl in the colder months, and pine-scented branches to welcome you home for the winter holidays.

The Elegant Tree

Even at Christmas, less can be more. If you would like a more toned-down look when it's time to decorate your tree, use only clear or all-white bulbs instead of the traditional varicolored ornaments and colored lights. Sprinkle the tree branches with powdered or crystal snow, and *voilà!* you'll have a beautiful, simply elegant tree.

Holiday Recycling

When the holidays are over, remove the branches from your Christmas tree and use them to fill your outdoor flower boxes and mulch the landscaped areas around the outside of your home.

Winter Green Flower Boxes for the Holidays

Plant four-inch Euro Pines in your flower boxes for a great holiday look that will last all winter. These mini-evergreens will look picture perfect whenever it snows, and when spring arrives, the pines can be transplanted into the ground to make room for your colorful annuals.

A Tree Alternative

If you are going out of town for Christmas and buying a tree is not in your plans, here's a festive alternative: Spray pine branches with faux snow or willow branches with textured red paint. Display them in a tall floor urn or in a smaller urn set on a pedestal. If you like, you can also hang tiny silver balls or Christmas cards from the branches to complete the look.

Christmas Quickies

Here are a few ways to give your home a few holiday accents without spending much money:

- Replace any candles you have displayed around the house with all red or all green ones.
- Place a big bowl filled with red apples or pomegranates on your dining-room table or entrance commode.
- Fill a large urn with evergreen branches that have pinecones attached (or attach loose pinecones with wire).
- Tape your holiday cards to a blank wall in the shape of a Christmas tree and add your own star on top. (There are now tapes available that can be removed without leaving a mark or taking paint with them, but you probably shouldn't try this on wallpaper!)

CHAPTER 14

Outer Beauty

Most homeowners devote substantial time and money to maintain the outside of their house—roofs, gutters, lawns, pavements, and the structure itself—in order to keep up appearances and the value of their property.

Whether you're concerned about "keeping up" with the neighbors or motivated by resale value alone, you can benefit from a few basic tips for making any house look better in a short period of time—assuming the lawn is green and mowed, and you've attended to all the basic repairs.

All the Trimmings

When painting the trim on the outside of windows and doors, take into consideration whether or not your house looks symmetrical and balanced or angular and out of balance when viewed from the street or road. If your home is already symmetrical, with a centered doorway flanked by an even number of windows on either side, you can paint the trim virtually any color that pleases you—whether it contrasts sharply with the rest of the house, or not. But if the structure is asymmetrical, you should try to keep the trim in the same color family as the rest of the exterior to create an effect that is more elegant and less visually jarring. If, for example, the house is painted cream, the trim might be a shade of taupe.

Outdoor Focus

Focal points are important on the outside of your home, too. When you look at your house from the street or road, does it feel balanced? Does it draw you in? Consider your landscaping. Do you have one ornamental tree or a symmetrical hedge lining the path or periphery of your property? Let the path on the side of your house lead to a garden, a stone pedestal with a sundial, or a decorative stone sculpture. In the center of the backyard, plant a unique tree or a bed of flowers. Any of these choices will serve as an attractive focal point and will make your property feel more pleasing and welcoming.

Thinking from the Outside In

The most elegant homes look pulled together on the outside as well as within. When you choose your indoor window treatments, think about how they will look from the outside as well. If you have different treatments in every room, the view from the outside of the house will be choppy, whereas uniform window dressings will create a smooth visual transition from window to window.

Whether you choose wooden blinds, pleated shades, or curtains, all the treatments on the first floor should be of the same material and color—at least as viewed from without. If you choose blinds or shades, you can still hang draperies to coordinate with your other fabrics; if you choose curtains, you can have them lined a uniform white or another light shade. There are many options that will give you flexibility within and uniformity without.

Uniformity Is Key

Just as you use one type of flowerpot or container for all your indoor plants, you should place all outdoor plants in just one type of holder and in one style pot or planter. For homes with porches, this applies to hanging plants, too.

Window Beautification

Create lush-looking all-weather window boxes by planting a row of long trailing plants, such as all-weather English Ivy, in the front row, and tall upright plants, such as geraniums, in the back row. The back row can be changed seasonally, while the front plants are left in place throughout the year.

Garbage In, Garbage Out

If you are forced to leave your garbage pails outside, be sure to build a covered bin to conceal them when they're not in use. A natural- or painted-wood container with a few open slates for ventilation is best, and, if space allows, plant some evergreens or shrubs around it.

You've Got Mail

Decorators know that every exterior detail is important because it is so exposed. Most people don't give something as apparently inconsequential as a crooked or badly painted mailbox a lot of thought, but it tells the world that the home behind it may not be cared for either.

Both the box and its post can be painted the same color as the trim on the house to create a customized look, or choose solid black or white for the mailbox.

Take time to paint your street number neatly on the box, or buy metal or wooden numbers to run down the post. Self-stick numbers look sloppy and are generally too large for the small surface of the mailbox. (See Resources.)

Pool and Patio

Match the color of your outdoor and pool furniture to the trim on your house, if possible, for a coordinated, elegant look.

If your trim is an unusual color that can't be matched, pick a neutral color or metal for the furniture that will blend with the color of the outside of the house.

Outdoor Arrangements

Where you place the furniture on your back deck is important not only because of the way it functions, but also because of the way it will look from the inside.

For example, if you place your dining-room table and chairs near the glass or French doors that look out on your deck, an outdoor table and chairs placed just beyond would seem heavy and redundant. To make the view more appealing and the deck seem more spacious, a better choice would be to place a pair of chaise lounges with a small table between them outside those doors. Then move the larger table and chairs farther away, preferably to a spot where you can't see them from the inside of the house.

An Indoor/Outdoor Alternative

If you don't have a family room or den but you do have a covered back porch, you can turn the porch into a comfortable, less formal alternative to the living room, if you choose furniture that suits the space.

Use wicker, rattan, or iron furniture with comfortable, thick cushions that will be cozy for chatting, reading, or daydreaming. And be sure to get a matching ottoman.

Purchase tables in the same finish to keep things looking pulled together, so that you'll have places to put down glassware, plates, and reading material.

An antique cookie jar filled with your favorite biscuits, a potted plant, and a few fluffy throw pillows that coordinate with the fabric on the seating will complete the look. If you have a heated porch or live in a warm climate, you can add one or two floor lamps with down-lights, in case you want to use the porch at night.

Flower Power

One of the designers with my firm always wanted a perennial flower garden, but her backyard did not get enough sunlight, and her front lawn was all landscaped and manicured, leaving no additional room for flowers. But wait, there was a tiny strip of land, 40" long by 20" wide, between the path next to her driveway and the tall hedge that marked her property line. Although it was an unorthodox spot for planting, she knew it would be perfect because it received full sun most of the day. She immediately started making plans for her dream garden. In went the peonies, roses, hydrangea, foxglove, and delphinium. In just a short time, the entire expanse was filled with colorful and fragrant blossoms, which now make her smile every morning and welcome her home in the evening.

A space that had been unutilized was suddenly enchanting and made to enhance the outside of our designer's home. In addition, thinking "outside of the box" helped her increase her property's value as well.

AstroTurf Alternatives

There are alternatives to that ubiquitous green indoor-and-outdoor carpeting for your terrace. Trex, for example, is a composition decking that will withstand all weather conditions. Or, you might check out Coral Springs neutrals, a durable outdoor carpeting. A natural teak deck kit links together in square shapes and can be disassembled when you move. Although not inexpensive, it provides years of use. (See Resources.)

Solution for All Seasons

Do you have a bricked-in or otherwise contained space in need of an airy, elegant look? Plant winter-hardy bamboo! This extremely fast-spreading, fast-growing plant looks wonderful year-round, in the heat of summer or with snow on the ground.

Walk as the Crow Flies

Traffic patterns count outside the house, too. If the pattern from your driveway to your front door is forcing people to waste steps, consider changing it.

Many builders, especially those of older homes, laid paths that made decorative statements but were totally impractical not only for arriving guests but for full-time residents as well.

If you have one of those roundabout sidewalks, try to lay a new path that will cut down the distance from the driveway or street to the front door.

Please, No Plastic Flamingos

Unless you have a small bungalow or country cabin, "cute" is not a word that should be used to describe the outside of your house.

Here are a few "decorative" items to avoid if you want your home to look refined:

- wind socks
- whirligigs
- lawn ornaments
- plastic outdoor accessories

When Form Follows Function

Outdoor decorations can serve a practical purpose at the same time they beautify your property. A prime example of this occurred when a famous movie actor and his wife bought an old farmhouse in rural Massachusetts and called us in for a consultation on ways to improve the grounds.

A slate path leading up to the pool area had one small step up to the pool's deck that was difficult to see. The actor was concerned that his children seemed to trip whenever they ran toward the pool, but he didn't want to rip out the old stonework because it had so much character.

As we walked around, I noticed an old metal arbor leaning against the barn. Although it was a bit rusty, it appeared to be in good condition. I suggested that they place the arbor over the problem step to delineate the area and serve as a reminder to the kids that there was a step they had to look out for.

"That works for me," he said. "My wife's been trying to figure out where we could put that pergola anyway, because she wants to plant morning glories that will grow up the sides. Our children will be safer, and we can use what we have to make my wife happy."

Resources

ALL ABOUT FURNITURE

Magic sliders are available at Bed Bath & Beyond, (www.bedbathandbeyond.com or 800–462–3966) and at better hardware stores.

The *narrow, upholstered bench,* made of wood, with a top upholstered in solid colored fabric, a hidden storage area under the seat, and casters for easy moving, is available from the Home Decorators Collection catalog (www.homedecorators.com or 800–245–2217). Or look at the selection of benches at Plow & Hearth Country Home (www.plowhearth.com or 800–627–1712).

A *round pedestal table* with leaves in the base (also available in rectangular shape), made by Skovby, is available from their catalog (www.skovby.dk), or from retailers such as Danish Design in New York City (212–223–7210).

An *upholstered headboard* that is five inches deep (the queen size is 64" wide by 48" high) and comes in a solid beige duck-cloth material is available from the Company Store catalogue (www.thecompanystore.com or 800–289–8508).

Finding a Place for Everything

A *wheeled cabinet* for the bathroom is available from Hold Everything (www.williams-sonomainc.com or 800–421–2285).

The *medicine cabinet* with mirror is available from Pottery Barn (www.potterybarn.com or 800–922–5507).

Home storage accessories are available from Hold Everything (www.williams-sonomainc.com or 800–421–2285), Kitchen Etc. (www.kitchenetc.com or 800–232–4070), or your local K-Mart store (www.bluelight.com).

The *canvas closet* is available from Hold Everything (www.williams-somomainc.com or 800–421–2285) or from Target stores (www.target.com).

Windows to the World

Roman, Matchstick, and Duette Shades with the "top-down, bottom-up" feature are available from Hunter Douglas. See your local dealer.

Wrinkle-free fabric relaxant is made by Westport Brands, Inc., Canton, Ohio. Available at better hardware stores.

Window sparkle cloth is made by the Cadie Company. Available at supermarkets and hardware stores.

Illuminating Solutions

Natural full spectrum light for seasonal affective disorder (SAD) is available in catalogs and from your local lighting store.

Decorating with Paint and Paper

Sure Grip® wallpaper adhesive. Call 732–469–8100 for your local source, or visit www.zinsser.com.

The Bottom Line on Flooring

Oil-based floor paint is made by Benjamin Moore (www.benjaminmoore.com or 888–236–6667) and Pratt and Lambert (www.prattandlambert.com or 800–BUY PRAT). Custom colors and readymade shades are available at decorator, home, hardware, and paint centers, including Janovic Plaza in New York City (212–772–1400), Home Depot (www.homedepot.com), or Lowes Home Centers (www.lowes.com) in your area.

Art, Accessories, and Finishing Touches

Invisible disc plate hangers are available from the Flatiron Disc Company (303–442–5586).

Wooden ledges for displaying art can be found in Exposures catalog (www.exposuresonline.com or 800–222–4947).

Hardware can be bought at Home Depot (www.homedepot.com), Lowes Home Centers (www.lowes.com), Restoration Hardware (www.restorationhardware.com), Rockler Woodworking & Hardware (www.rockler.com or 800–279–4441); and most hardware, design, and home stores offer extensive selections in a wide range of prices.

Simple Solutions for Kitchens and Baths

Stock replacement doors are at the Home Depot (www.homedepot.com), Lowes Home Centers (www.lowes.com), or IKEA (www.ikea.com) in your area.

The *breakfast bar,* with a stainless-steel top, is practical for preparing food as well as for eating. Available through the Williams-Sonoma catalog (www.williams-sonomainc.com or 800–541–2233). Similar items are available through DeliverAll.com or Kitchen Etc. (www.kitchenetc.com).

The *collapsible serving cart with wheels and shelf,* in black, white, or chrome, is available from Bloomingdale's (www.bloomingdales.com) or Kitchen Etc. (www.kitchenetc.com). They fold closed to three inches in width for easy storage—a good investment if you entertain often.

The *Rain Shower showerhead* is available at fine hardware stores everywhere or online at www.faucet.com.

A *narrow sink shelf* is available at Home Depot (www.homedepot.com) or Pottery Barn (www.potterybarn.com or 800–922–5507).

HOME OFFICES

All kinds of office furniture:

Design within Reach: www.dwr.com or 800–944–2233

Home Decorators Collection: www.homedecorators.com or 800–245–2217

Horchow Home: 800–456–7000

Reliable Home Office: www.reliable.com or 800–869–6000

Levengers: www.levenger.com or 800–544–0880

Crate and Barrel: www.crateandbarrel.com or 800–323–5461

The *wire-cover kit* that enables you to cut a black or white cord cover to the length you desire is available from Hold Everything (www.williams-sonomainc.com or 800–421–2264).

THE FAMILY-FRIENDLY HOME

Kids' closets are available at Pottery Barn Kids (www.potterybarn.com or 800–922–9934).

Kitchen stools with backs are available at Pottery Barn (www.potterybarn.com or 800–922–9934) or Crate and Barrel (www.crateandbarrel.com or 800–323–5461). The Spiegel catalog also carries a variety of stools (www.spiegel.com or 800–527–1577 to order a catalog).

The *Scald Safe faucet* is available at better hardware stores or through www.faucet.com.

BRINGING THE OUTDOORS IN

The *Asian-style fountain* can be purchased in many stores and from catalogs such as Smith & Hawken (www.smith-hawken.com or 800–776–3336).

Change for All Seasons

Fans can be found at the Modern Fan Company (www.modernfan.com), Casablanca Fan Company (www.casablancafanco.com) for both modern and traditional styles, and Hunter Fan Company (www.hunterfan.com) for traditional styles.

The *Cinni table fan* is from Pottery Barn The (www.potterybarn.com or 800–922–5507).

The *Wind Chaser Pedestal Floor Fan* is available at Brookstone (www.brookstone.com or 800–846–3000).

Vornado's Silver Swan is available at Bed Bath & Beyond (www.bedbathandbeyond.com or 800–462–3966).

The *faux fur throw* is available from Fabulous Furs (www.fabulousfurs.com or 800–848–4650). These large (72" x 53") "skins" come in twelve varieties of "fur" and are lined in velour. They range in price from $139 to $299.

Outer Beauty

Copper and bronze doorbells and other distinctive hardware are available from Rocky Mountain Hardware. Check online at www.rockymountainhardware.com or call 888–788–2013 for a catalog or location of local dealers.

Astro Turf, durable outdoor carpeting made by Norman D. Liston Company, is available in oatmeal or a combination of black, white, and gray; a combination of ginger-brown and off-white; and a navy and blue/green combination. It comes in twelve-foot widths. Check with your local dealer for details.

The *teak deck kit* is available from the Smith & Hawken catalog, 800–776–3336.

Trex Easy Care Decking is a composite material made from recycled wood and plastic bags and looks like gray weathered wood. Check www.trex.com to find the dealer in your area.

Index

F

Fabrics, 15
    cat clawing of, 143–144
Family-friendly home, 133
    bathroom safety, 137
    bulletin board, 137
    closets that grow with child,
        135
    converting nursery to child's
        room, 134
    covering cat-torn upholstery
        when entertaining, 144
    easy-wipe wallpaper, 136
    fabrics cats love to claw,
        143–144
    humidifier alternatives, 143
    pet booties, 146
    reclaiming adult space, 142
    removing pet stains and
        odors from carpet, 146
    replacing coat rack with
        wall-mounted hooks,
        142
    safe seating prevents falls,
        137
    Scald Safe faucet, 140
    Shoji screens as room
        dividers, 140–141
    shower-curtain liner tuck-in
        reminder, 143
    sibling sanity, 136
    simple furniture, 136
    sleeping loft for small
        bedroom, 145
    slip-free flooring, 140
    soothing colors, 136
    storage under platform bed,
        134–135
    three-way switches on table
        lamps, 143
    toddler safety, 134

touch latch magnetic
    hardware, 140
toy avalanche, 138–139
trundle bed for sleepovers,
    135
upstairs open railing, 140
Family heirlooms, 14
Family room, must-haves, 36
Faux-fur throw, 164
Faux paint treatments, 76
Finials, 66
Finishing touches
    antique romance, 105–106
    dust ruffle decor, 106–107
    matching metals, 105
Fireplace, 102
    alternative, 165
Flair-arm sofa, 20
Flat finish paint, 73–74
Flooring, 79
    carpeting
        area rug over wall-to-wall,
            87
        in bedroom, 87
        commercial for high-
            traffic areas, 86
        fiber types, 85
        in hallway to bedroom, 89
        measuring wall-to-wall,
            86
        one per room, 87
        removing in warm
            weather, 87
        square in round room,
            88–89
        types of, 85–86
    kitchen, 110–111
    wood
        alternatives to, 82–84
        care of, 81–82
        in dining room, 85
        nonslip, 84, 140

protecting, 84
replacement alternatives,
    84–85
staining, 80–81
Flower arrangements, 150,
    154–156
Focal point, 10, 15, 102
    outdoor, 170
Formica, 114
Fountains, 150
Frosted bulbs, 64
Frosted glass, 59
Full-spectrum light, 64
Furniture
    basic rules for, 13–14
    bedroom space, 33
    bedside tables, 32–34
    casters/wheels on, 28
    for children, 136
    coffee tables, end tables, 24
    cushions, 21
    desk into dressing table, 25
    dining-room tables/chairs,
        27
    end tables, 24
    European pillows, 33
    family heirlooms, 14
    flexible, 26
    focal point, 15
    glass tops for, 25
    glass-top tables, 22
    hardware
        original, 28
        transforming, 29
    headboards, 33
    inherited, 31
    loveseats, 23
    marble for existing wood
        top, 29–30
    metal elements, 32
    mixing and matching, 14–15
    moving, 34

You can transform your entire

home with Lauri Ward's

Use What You Have® Decorating.

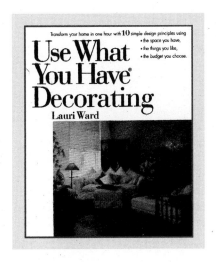

Now available in paperback wherever books are sold.

For more information about the Interior Refiners Network (Decorator Training Program), consultations, and seminars, please visit www.redecorate.com or call 800-WE-USE-IT.